PRAISE FOR ACTIVATOR

"How do you know what really works in leadership? Read this book to find out. Jones bases his recommendations on leading-edge brain science and provides a plethora of actionable ideas you can use to become an activator."
 — **Mark Sanborn**, President of Sanborn & Associates, Inc. and best-selling author of *You Don't Need a Title to be a Leader* and *The Intention Imperative*

"A very interesting and insightful read. Jones is an innovative voice in our new world of work. Read it and take your leadership to the next level!"
 — **Marshall Goldsmith**, New York Times #1 best-selling author of *Triggers, Mojo, and What Got You Here Won't Get You There*

"Take this to heart. This book will help you unleash the best in your people and take their performance to the next level!"
 — **Paul Stoltz,** CEO of Peak Learning, Inc. and best-selling Author of *GRIT*

"Dr. Jones is one of the true experts in the field of motivational psychology. The insights found in this book will help anyone become a better leader, colleague, and teammate in an ever-changing and more interconnected world."
 — **Maggi Reiss**, President, IDS Publishing Corporation

"Jason shares how this Activator approach is more effective based on the way our brains work. This book provides excellent tactics business leaders can use to motivate their employees to achieve their highest level of performance. This is a must-read for managers who want to help their employees reach their true potential."
 — **Jeff Kilpartick,** CEO of EGW Utilities

"Imagine using the power of brain science to take your organization to the next level. Let Jason Jones empower you with the latest principles of leadership and help you implement practical techniques to unleash the best in your people."

—**Dr. Michelle Adams**, Founder and President, Marketing Brainology

"Activator is a breath of fresh air for leaders who want to grow. Jason provides a simple, but not easy, path to truly deepen the engagement of those I lead. His insights in this book, backed by science, challenged me as a leader while providing a clear path to help me truly understand what motivates those around me After reading Activator, I realize that I'm not as good at connecting with others as I think I am. A prediction called out in Chapter six of the book. But Jason does not leave you stuck. He provides a path to a journey for continuous improvement…if you're willing to take it."

— **Steve Shoemaker**, President, Ideal Homes and Neighborhoods

"Jason is a coach, connector, and culture cognizant leader that shares proven scientific principles with practical application that will light up your leadership and activate your performance. You will lead with more energy, integrity, and results, and you will understand what motivates others to do the same."

— **Dr. Ronda Beaman,** Professor, Cal Poly State University and Director of Leadership Studies

"Dr. Jason Jones delivers the context for leadership in this important look on becoming an Activator. When we take the time to understand who we work with and what motivates us, we take an important step forward in our leadership journeys. This insightful book will be an excellent addition to any leader's toolkit."

— **Scott Mueller,** Sr. Vice President, Organizational Development, MidFirst Bank

"The world is full of "how-to's" for improving communication, leadership, and performance. But rarely do you find that proper blend of practical execution combined with an understanding of how the human brain truly works. Jason presents a complicated subject matter, with immediate and practical implementation strategies. A must-read for anyone looking to communicate better, have more in-depth, stronger relationships, and excel at leading and motivating those around them."
— **Jeremy Edwards**, CEO of Raremark

"Dr. Jones has raised the bar when it comes to activating our greatest potential. Backed by the science but wrapped in the art of dealing with people this book is a must-read. You will want to have your highlighter ready because every chapter is filled with information you need to know. Regardless of our title, tenure, or role, this book will help you unlock your Activator skills to help you personally, professionally, and even organizationally."
— **Tony Bridwell,** Chief People Officer, Culture Architect, International Speaker, and Best- Selling Author of *Saturday Morning Tea* and the *Maker Series*

"This book is a must read for leaders and professionals interested in understanding and unlocking the true potentials of others. Dr. Jones leverages cutting edge brain science and motivation theory to provide practical and actionable insights for all leaders and professionals."
— **Mike Reiss** President, IDS Publishing Corporation

"Dr. Jason Jones takes a new look at going beyond traditional employee engagement. His deep research on how employees are activated through brain science will give you an advantage in crafting the right culture. This book will help you understand true leadership by facilitating the success of others."
— **Gene Hammett**, Bestselling author of *The Trap of Success*, host of *Growth Think Tank* podcast

"Over the past decade, I have had the opportunity to work alongside Dr. Jones on numerous occasions. Jason draws from a deep reservoir of academic preparation, professional experience and possesses a sincere passion for helping people and organizations thrive. This book represents Dr. Jones at his best, taking complex concepts and presenting them in a way that is inspiring, practical and useful."

— **Dr. Nathan Mellor**, CEO of Strata Leadership and author of *Sleeping Giants*

"Dr. Jason Jones has uncovered the key to becoming the type of leader who brings out the best in others – helping them reach their full potential. Based on the latest research in brain science and motivation, this book encapsulates what you, as a leader, need to learn in order to develop your people, growing their ability to think and do, and empowering them to passionately achieve more than they ever thought possible. Even though this book is based on theory that is proven out through research, it is highly practical and easy to understand and apply, giving you what you need to inspire and creatively engage with your employees. Be prepared to be changed and empowered, yourself, as you incorporate what you learn from this captivating read."

— **Dr. Virginia Smith**, Senior Director, Institutional Effectiveness and Accreditation, Oklahoma State University — Oklahoma City.

"Jason blends the latest scientific insights with practical action steps and stories. With masterful precision, he delivers the most useful book I've seen on this topic."

— **Bruce McIntyre**, CEO of the Parkinson Foundation of Oklahoma and Author of *Thrive Anyway*

"Jason has crafted a detailed look at culture and employee engagement in this book. I tend to lead more by feel but Jason brings to light a helpful structure and explains the science behind the "feel." It is invaluable to understand why it works and it will allow me to be more consistent as a leader."

— **Frank Smith**, President, Mosaic Personnel Solutions and Driving Happiness at Work

ACTIVAT⏻R

USING BRAIN SCIENCE TO BOOST MOTIVATION, DEEPEN ENGAGEMENT, AND SUPERCHARGE PERFORMANCE

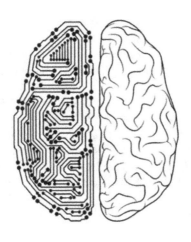

Jason E. Jones, Ph.D.

Cataloging-in-Publication Data is on file at the Library of Congress

Publisher's Cataloging-in-Publication data
Names: Jones, Jason E., author.
Title: Activator : using brain science to boost motivation , deepen engagement , and supercharge performance / Jason E. Jones, Ph.D.
Description: Dallas, TX: Bright House Press, 2021.
Identifiers: LCCN: 2020922901 | ISBN 978-0-9894719-5-4 (Hardcover) | 978-0-9894719-3-0 (pbk.) | 978-0-9894719-4-7 (e-book)
Subjects: LCSH Leadership. | Motivation. | Success in business. | Organizational effectiveness. | Personnel management. | Employee motivation. | BISAC BUSINESS & ECONOMICS / Management | BUSINESS & ECONOMICS / Workplace Culture | BUSINESS & ECONOMICS / Leadership.
Classification: LCC HD57.7 .J66 2021 | DDC 658.4--dc23

Hardcover ISBN: 978-0-9894719-5-4
Softcover ISBN: 978-0-9894719-3-0
e-book ISBN: 978-0-9894719-4-7

1st edition, February 2021

Printed in the United States of America

To my amazing kids, Millie, Owen, and Brock who have given me a reason to be a better person every day and to do my best to make the world a better place.

CONTENTS

INTRODUCTION   1

    Choosing How We Lead   4
    How To Read This Book   5

PART I RETHINKING WORKPLACE
MOTIVATION & ENGAGEMENT   7
Chapter 1 The Bandwagon Workplace   9

    The Next Step Forward   13

Chapter 2 What Really Motivates   15

    The Three Human Drives   18
    Brain Anatomy And Drive   23
    New Perspectives On Motivation   25
    The Emergence Of Brain Science   27

PART II THE NEW SCIENCE OF PERFORMANCE   29
Chapter 3 The Performance Pathway   31

    Motivation's Secret Sauce   33
    Leading High Performance   38

Chapter 4 Lighting-Up The Brain   43

    The Neuroscience Of Leadership   48
    Brain Science Basics   49

Chapter 5 Becoming An Activator   55

    The Internal Mechanism Of Motivation   59
    The External Mechanism Of Motivation   63
    Frame The Environment   66
    Becoming An Activator   70
    Activator Skills   71

PART III ACTIVATION SKILLS   75
Chapter 6 Connecting   77

Cultivating Trust Through Relationships   77
The 3 Elements Of Connection   84
Activation Words   94
Constructive Communication   97
Activation Phrases   98
Connecting Motivation   99
Brain Activation - Connecting Tactics   108

Chapter 7 Coaching   113

Facilitating High-Performance With Backbone And Heart   113
What Kind Of Coach Are You?   114
Leading With Backbone And Heart   118
The Goal Model   122
Coaching Skills   127
Coaching Tips   141
Coaching Employee Growth And Development   143
Brain Activation - Coaching Tactics   146

Chapter 8 Culturing   151

Setting And Upholding Standards Of Excellence   151
The 3 Levels Of Engagement   155
Frame Your Culture   159
Brain Activation - Culturing Tactics   180

Chapter 9 Activator Development   189
Apendix A   195
Acknowledgements   203
End Notes   205
About The Author   213

INTRODUCTION

Several hundred business leaders and celebrities were invited to the unveiling of the Tesla Roadster at Barker Hangar in Santa Monica, California, on July 19, 2006. Elon Musk and Martin Eberhard introduced Tesla Motors' first car as the future of vehicles and explained its superiority over gas-powered vehicles. Attendees were then allowed to test drive the car on the airport's expansive runway. Afterward, Eberhard and Musk invited the audience to be a part of an exclusive group called the "Signature One Hundred." Membership in this elite circle was offered for $100,000 to the first one hundred buyers. For this handsome sum, each member would receive a Signature One Hundred Special Edition Roadster, to be delivered by the following summer. The pitch was successful. Over the next two weeks, Tesla took orders for 126 and launched an electric car company.

The Tesla story is intriguing, even more so because it is full of myths. For instance, many believe Elon Musk started the company and gave it the name Tesla. The truth is that the company was founded by Martin Eberhard and Marc Tarpenning in July 2003. It wasn't until a year later that Musk became an early investor and, in 2008, assumed the role of chairman. Another myth is that Tesla invented electric vehicle technology, and the July 2006 launch in Santa Monica was the birth of the electric car. It wasn't. Electric cars have been on the road for more than a hundred years before Tesla Motors was launched.

In fact, they were the most popular type of vehicle in the late 1800s. At that time, battery technology was rapidly advancing and revolutionizing how people moved from place to place.

The first battery-powered vehicle debuted around 1890 when a chemist from Des Moines, Iowa, created a six-passenger car (more like a wagon, really) with a top speed of fourteen miles per hour. The next two decades were marked by great advancement in battery and electric vehicle technologies thanks to the work of Thomas Edison, Ferdinand Porsche, and countless other chemists and engineers. Porsche became well known for selling an electric car called the P1 in 1898.[1] But then something interesting happened.

The future of electric cars was derailed in 1908 when the Ford Motor Company introduced the Model T. Almost overnight, the gasoline-powered engine became the favored vehicle engine and battery-powered vehicles faded away. Why? That answer is easy. Ford's gas-powered vehicle was introduced at half the price of a battery-powered vehicle. Gasoline, at the time, was also cheap and plentiful. Nobody had a clue that combustion engines would one day create environmental issues. So for more than a hundred years, the world harnessed the power of the gasoline engine in ways prior generations could not have imagined. Meanwhile, the science and technology of battery-powered transportation largely remained in the archives.

Let's stop here. This book is not about cars or technology. Nor am I trying to convince you to buy an electric vehicle. Tesla's brilliance isn't found in the discovery of electric and battery technology. It is in their vision and ability to harness it. The core science was there for the taking. Musk and Eberhard saw the benefits of harnessing such power and were willing to invest hard work upfront to reap great rewards down the road.

When given a choice, we opt for what we believe to be the easiest, quickest, and cheapest path to our goal. Then when we commit to an approach, we become biased towards it. In the case of transportation, we were alerted to the pollution caused by combustion exhaust in the early 1950s, but the use of gasoline engines continued to increase. The 1970s oil embargo temporarily took gas prices through the roof, yet automobile makers continued to produce gas-powered cars. Even though science and technology were available to leverage battery power and grow its capability, we defaulted to the easier, faster, and cheaper route. Now, several decades later, with the help of Tesla, people believe in the viability of electric cars and the need for a better approach.

The choice made decades ago for powering our cars is similar to the choice we make today for how we power our people. For far too many years, leaders have chosen what they believe to be the easy, fast, and cheap way to lead and influence. Leaders believed that threats, coercion, manipulation, authority, and incentives create the motivation that drives loyalty and high performance. Yet a growing set of data shows that our beliefs have been wrong. The popular approach wasn't easy, fast, and cheap. It turns out to have been hard, slow, and expensive.

There is a better way—a way that has been validated by science and is right here, in front of us, ready to be harnessed. This approach to leadership generates higher levels of engagement and achievement than we ever thought possible. It's more efficient and cost-effective, too. I haven't even mentioned the best thing about the "fuel" that powers this system—it's renewable!

CHOOSING HOW WE LEAD

The data regarding employee engagement, job satisfaction, and performance reveals a dirty secret that many organizations don't want to face—there has been a lack of effective leadership for many decades. How do I know this? Take a look at any of the thousands of employee surveys that are conducted each year, and you will find that most people hate their job, loathe going to work, feel unappreciated, and report high levels of stress each day.

Eighty-three percent of workers suffer from work-related stress.[2] Thirty-five percent of employees say their main source of stress is their manager. This stress results in roughly sixty-three percent of employees wishing they could quit their jobs. Sixty percent report that they have quit a prior job due to a bad manager.[3]

To make matters worse, stress leads to poor health, which inhibits performance. According to the Center for Workplace Mental Health, work-related stress causes 120,000 deaths and results in $190 billion in healthcare costs annually.[4] Lost productivity due to workplace-induced health problems costs organizations more than $84 billion annually.[5] Something is wrong with the way we are working and the responsibility falls on the shoulders of those who lead.

This is an issue we cannot ignore. We can do better. As leaders, we are uniquely positioned to make a significant impact on the people we lead and change the unfortunate state of today's working environment.

In this book, I explain the implications of the most recent scientific studies on effective leadership and offer ways you can apply their principles in your daily experience. I'll guide you through the steps to evaluate your leadership approach, show you how to root out the behaviors that are hindering your success, and teach you how to motivate and engage your people. Along the way, I will share with you dozens of ways to activate the brains of the people you lead, to bring out the best in them.

HOW TO READ THIS BOOK

I wrote this book to be as concise as possible. At some points, I'll spend a little extra time helping you understand the science that drives the approach. While it might seem like more background than you need, I encourage you to give those sections a try, so you can have a deeper appreciation for how the brain functions and *why* this approach works. It will equip you to create tactics that are specific to your situation. My goal is to help you acquire the necessary information and skills quickly so you can immediately start activating your people.

Before you begin this journey, I want to let you know that I have created a companion resource for this book. I can't pack everything I would like into this book, so I have created a website—TheActivatorBook.com—to give you the additional resources, tools, and bonuses referenced throughout the book. These resources will help you incorporate the ideas of this book into your daily leadership behavior.

This book is separated into three parts. Part one, the first two chapters, challenges you to rethink outdated beliefs related to motivation and engagement in the workplace. Our ability to grow and develop as leaders hinges on our willingness to evaluate our thoughts and behaviors and determine whether we're getting the outcomes we desire. Such reflection is necessary to innovate and evolve to meet the ever-changing needs of the people and culture we lead. I encourage you to take a fresh approach to how you lead. These chapters will help you explore the latest science, what it says about why people behave in certain ways and provide you with a clear path forward.

Part two, chapters 3 through 5, guides you through the elements of the new science of performance. We'll take a deep dive into the latest behavioral and brain research and apply it to your leadership style. In chapter four, I introduce you to the "Activation" approach that will give you the mindset and skill-set needed to lead more effectively. This section will help you understand what you can do to raise the ceiling of potential for your people and unleash them from the factors that have hindered their energy and enjoyment in their work.

The third and final part of this book, chapters 6 through 9, will help you build and practice the three Activator Skills. I suggest more than seventy tactics that you can use to supercharge the brains of the people you lead. As you implement the tactics provided for each skill, you will see your people flourish and thrive.

Finally, I end the book with a chapter focused on your growth and development as an Activator. Your ability to invest in others can only be as strong as your investment in yourself. While Activators are mentally and emotionally strong, this approach requires that, you take care of yourself, manage your own brain health, and continually grow as a person.

My goal is to give you easy-to-understand information and explanations so you can apply these tactics to your unique situation. While I will share proven principles and ideas, your challenge is to apply them to your daily leadership behavior. That is the real work of leadership. Approaches and strategies are helpful, but the true measure of success is how you apply them to the needs of *your* people.

PART I

RETHINKING WORKPLACE MOTIVATION & ENGAGEMENT

CHAPTER 1
THE BANDWAGON WORKPLACE

If you were alive during the early-to-mid 1800s and wanted a deeper understanding of your personality, character, and aptitude, you might have sought the help of a phrenologist. The field of Phrenology studied the shape of a person's head to predict their mental traits—including personality, character, and intelligence—to promote better health and self-knowledge. The field gained significant support as a legitimate science in the early nineteenth century based on the writings of Franz Joseph Gall, a German physician who specialized in the anatomy and physiology of the nervous system. Gall created a map showing how twenty-seven individual organs of the body correspond to regions within the brain to determine personality. His unique method of examining patients noted the bumps and indentations on their heads to make psychological diagnoses. After Gall's death in 1828, Johann Gaspar Spurzheim popularized the term phrenology and spread the practice throughout Europe and North America.[1]

It wasn't until the 1840s that phrenology was discredited as a scientific theory and medical practitioners took a negative view on it. When we look back on the phrenology era today, we can clearly see its flaws. It was pseudoscience—a practice presented as scientifically proven but was, in fact, incompatible with science. However, during that time phrenology was a novel concept and seemed plausible. Its principles were communicated persuasively by the practitioners who used it, and the promise that it held—to unlock the secrets of the human psyche—was irresistible.

Phrenology benefited from a phenomenon called the Bandwagon Effect, whereby the acceptance of an idea or belief increases with respect to the proportion of others who have already done so. Trends are birthed from the Bandwagon Effect, and most humans can't resist jumping on board. The workplace isn't immune to bandwagons.

Employee engagement has been one of the biggest trends in organizations over the past two decades. Companies have poured billions of dollars into their efforts to boost motivation and increase engagement in hopes that a fully committed workforce will deliver lower operational costs and higher profitability. Yet the unfortunate reality is that the data doesn't show any improvement on this measure over the past twenty years. As a whole, business leaders have realized no significant return on all that time and money invested.

EMPLOYEE ENGAGEMENT TREND (U.S.)

Annual Averages

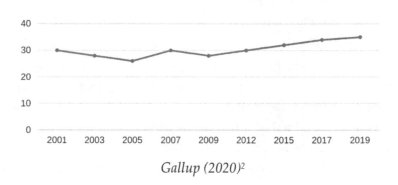

Gallup (2020)[2]

A quick look at the chart shows only a slight rise in employee engagement in the United States between 2001 and 2019. When accounting for statistical error and economic variables, the rise is nominal and perhaps nonexistent. It's even worse around the world as only 15% of workers say they are highly involved and enthusiastic about their work.[3] According to Gallup, 70% of employees don't like their job, and half are looking for another place to work. They also estimate that the cost of disengagement to organizations in the U.S. is approximately $605 billion annually.[4]

While I don't want to be perceived as a negative nelly, I do want to highlight the issue so we can leverage what we have done well and evolve to be more effective at leading our people. It's easy for anyone to fall into the trap of blind and assumptive beliefs when everyone is doing it. We think if the vast majority of people are doing something a certain way, then it must be the right way. And yes, a healthy culture is a worthy goal for any organization, but many assumptions have been made on how to achieve it. As many leaders become aware of their lack of progress, they logically ask, *"After all the surveying, action-planning, and activities we have invested in, why haven't our engagement score risen significantly?"*

Building a loyal and high-performing culture is important, yet it's tricky. Trying to determine exactly what organizational factors will move the needle is a complex, but worthy task, as so many of our desired outcomes hinge on the commitment and behaviors of employees. Gallup's annual State of the American Workplace Reports highlights key metrics that are impacted by employee satisfaction levels. One recent report found that companies with high levels of engagement also have 59% less turnover, 17% higher productivity, 20% higher sales, and 41% lower absenteeism. Gallup also reports that companies with highly engaged employee cultures outperform other companies by 202%.[4]

The promise of pulling the engagement lever and receiving the reward of lower turnover and high-performance seems like a no-brainer. However, having led culture strategy in a large organization and helping many companies create these strategies as a consultant, I can tell you without a doubt that solving this problem is more than a process of identifying a gap and filling it.

The reality is that we are working with humans who carry with them many intertwining factors that impact commitment level. Many of these factors are difficult to understand, isolate, and measure. Robert Bacal, author of the book *Performance Management*, calls these influencers, "micro factors." A micro factor can be anything that supports or hinders a person's willingness to engage.[5] These factors include employee's attitude, personality, ambitions, mental health, job duties, and work relationship interactions. Companies and their leaders have little control over these elements. The image below illustrates the multitude of factors that influence engagement on a daily basis. Notice the items you can control and those that you can't.

THE NEXT STEP FORWARD

While employee surveying can provide helpful insights, it's important that leaders understand that engagement measurement is data only. When analyzed well and with the right expectations, it can serve the organization, offering a better understanding of important strengths, weaknesses, opportunities, and threats. However, increasing commitment and ownership among your people starts with creating a cultural strategy that leverages the most powerful influencer—leaders.

According to the best data available on engagement, a leader's interactions with their employee is the most critical component impacting that person's choice to commit to an organization's goals and put extra effort into helping achieve them. Gallup's research shows that managers account for at least 70% of the variance in employee engagement scores.[6] Employees respond positively to leaders who are caring, fair, supportive, and use corresponding tactics. A study conducted by Ultimate Software and Generational Kinetics found that more than half of employees surveyed would turn down a 10% pay raise to stay with a great leader.[7] A positive employee-manager relationship doesn't guarantee motivation or high performance, but knowing the level of impact that this relationship carries should prompt every organization to invest in this over other programs and activities designed to boost employee satisfaction.

The data suggests that we ought to approach human-capital goals more holistically. We must use systemic thinking and put culture development into context with micro-factors, including the individual differences and unique needs of people. This approach also helps us understand and leverage the environment that people work in and the significant effect it has on their behavior.

A new approach is required, and it must fit the needs of employees in the twenty-first century. It's time to reevaluate our old, outdated strategies and refresh our understanding of human behavior in the workplace. It's time to build on what has worked and evolve toward a science-based, yet practical, approach to workplace motivation, engagement, and performance. To do this, we need to take a step back and get a clearer understanding of what the latest science says about what really motivates people to act with commitment.

CHAPTER 2
WHAT REALLY MOTIVATES

I often hear people interchange the words motivation and engagement. Most people think they are synonymous and don't understand the importance of their differentiation. Motivation is a person's psychological energy to do something (to act). It is deeply internal, and the energy is derived from our deepest physiological and psychological needs and values. Engagement, on the other hand, is a broad measure of a person's commitment-oriented behaviors. The distinction is critical to understand because all employees are motivated, but when their motivation isn't aligned or supported by the activities in their workplace, they don't fully engage. A person can be motivated but not engaged. But a person must be motivated to be engaged. Motivation serves as the critical energy that drives engaged behavior. Motivation is the essential energy that fuels our action to meet our needs, achieve our goals, and lead a satisfying life. Let's take a few minutes to understand how a leader can energize or drain a follower's motivation.

I loved my job! But that changed almost overnight. Several years ago, I worked for a well-run, solid company. I had a role that was, for that point in my career, a dream job. I had built a team of people that were good at their work. We made a positive impact on the company and were progressively improving and innovating. We surpassed all of our performance goals and targets. The team had an extremely positive outlook on what we would achieve in the coming months and years. In a meeting with my team, I praised their hard work and ingenuity. At that point, I asked confidently—and rhetorically—"What can stop us?"

Within a few weeks, I found the answer to that question. And not only did it stop us, it derailed an entire team's performance, engagement, and perception of the company. The catalyst of this derailing was our leader. He was a new hire who replaced my previous manager. While his resume contained stints at notable companies, it was obvious from the dates on his LinkedIn profile that he had not stayed at any organization for more than two-and-a-half years over the preceding decade. It was a red flag, but I decided I would give him the benefit of the doubt, and I looked forward to our first one-on-one meeting.

I sat across the table from him. After some pleasantries, he asked for an overview of my projects, metrics, and prior successes. I confidently reviewed each program and my team's current projects, along with budgets. He shook his head and grunted several times.

I expected him to praise the work, but he didn't. I distinctly remember him not making eye contact with me for a long time while he looked over the project documents and wrote notes in his notebook. Then he said, "Let me tell you what we did at my last company." He spent the next fifteen minutes telling me how each of my programs and projects could be improved. He told me all the things he would have expected to see in each project but didn't. His tone of voice and statements insinuated that the project plan, and its execution, was below his expectations. He didn't congratulate, praise, or even acknowledge the hard work my team and I had done over the prior two years. I felt deflated. Even worse, I left the meeting feeling disrespected and misunderstood.

Unfortunately, that was just the beginning. Over the following weeks, my work, and the work of my employees, was scrutinized and belittled. Unsurprisingly, the dynamic of my team changed. Because they worked closely with my supervisor, they became visibly stressed and lost enthusiasm for their work. They tried to avoid him in the hallway and break room. I found myself in constant repair mode, trying to fix or reframe his poor attempts at constructive feedback, which were perceived as criticisms or threats.

About two months into this new reality, one of my employees called me to discuss a situation that had occurred. When I met face-to-face with her, I could see that her eyes were red. She was angry, hurt, and embarrassed. She told me that my supervisor had stopped by her desk and delivered a list of criticisms on her performance. Not only had he done this without an ounce of care, his list of grievances had been delivered within earshot of another colleague. As you can imagine, I was both angered at how she had been treated and annoyed that he had done this without consulting me.

By the time my team and I had reached the three-month mark under this leader, we were all looking for new jobs. Where before, we had tackled projects with excitement, by that point our daily work had become an unpleasant grind. We questioned the trust we had placed in the company, because their standards of leadership conduct—which they supposedly valued—were not being upheld. Day-after-day we witnessed our leader not being held accountable for his poor management practices.

Sadly, that leader was completely oblivious to the negative impact of his behavior. He couldn't grasp how his interactions with people were causing morale to plummet. When he saw performance stagnating, he blamed me and then used demands and threats to push us harder. All the while, he perceived himself to be a highly competent and effective leader.

Far from motivating the people working under him, this leader drove them away. Within a year, the majority of my team had left the company. It's a sad case study of how poor leadership can adversely impact an organization and the lives of its people. Too many leaders continue to use antiquated approaches to leadership that rely upon intimidation, positional power, and control to get the behaviors they want. That old model of leadership triggers the brain's survival and reward instincts. They may produce quick results, but they damage an employee's willingness to give their best on their own accord and over the long-term.

THE THREE HUMAN DRIVES

Throughout history, leaders have mostly relied on two of the three deeply rooted human drives that move people to action. These two drives respond to threats, manipulation, and coercion. We have all read the poignant methods leaders and dictators have used to get the behaviors they desire from the people they lead. Those that use this style of leadership rely only on the most primitive part of the brain to get the response they want. To better understand why leaders have employed these tactics, let's take a quick look at the three drivers of motivation and their respective brain functions.

A drive is our basic—sometimes automatic—instinct to take action in our favor. Each is "hardwired" into our brains, and they energize our desire to monitor our environment and take the necessary actions to meet our personal needs. While every human has these three drives, each person's genetic makeup and life experiences can alter their level of sensitivity.

SURVIVAL DRIVE

The Survival Drive is your brain's response to physical or psychological threats. The most fundamental job of your brain is to keep you alive and safe. The "fight or flight" response is one well-known example of how the Survival Drive supports your need for safety. It can also activate autonomic functions such as hormone and neurochemical production and release. While evoking the Survival Drive is often the fastest way to ensure obedience, it will never foster self-directed compliance in anyone. People rebel against leaders who rely on this for motivation. Eventually they will revolt and fight to gain a sense of safety and freedom.

Leaders who threaten or use fear tactics at work often employ the use of power and authority derived from a their title or position. A leader doesn't have to threaten a person's life to elicit a survival response. The human brain interprets any threat as an attack on its survival and responds accordingly. An example of this is a production line manager telling an employee that he will be fired after one more mistake.

While this kind of motivation is still prevalent, many companies are equipping their leaders to move away from this strategy. Hierarchy and positional power can bring value to a workplace when used appropriately to ensure accountability and operational control. However, leaders who use fear-based tactics to achieve these ends will create a culture of rebellion and disengagement.

REWARD DRIVE

The Reward Drive is your brain's response to reward, reinforcement, and punishment. It deciphers pleasure and pain and determines your response to it. If something is pleasurable or you expect it to be, you may generate energy for that behavior. If your brain perceives the experience or reinforcement as painful, you're more likely to avoid it. Unsurprisingly, reward-based systems and incentive programs seek to activate the energy that this drive creates.

In the research of B.F. Skinner, a famous Harvard psychologist in the mid-twentieth century, he noted that rewards have become a staple of modern motivation. Skinner's research showed that rewarded behaviors have a higher likelihood of being repeated.

Research studies conducted over the past few decades have shown that rewards and incentives can boost performance in some situations, but they are likely to be short-lived and can undermine intrinsic motivation — where people find enjoyment in their work. An example of this would be a manager who tells her team that she will give a bonus to each person who achieves their sales goal. Research also shows that using rewards can produce lower-quality motivation and lead to lower levels of self-regulation and discipline on the part of the person who is being rewarded.

Companies that leverage rewards to motivate behavior must be careful about how they use this method. Leaders who use reward haphazardly will often create a sense of entitlement on the part of employees. When rewards aren't achieved employee motivation and loyalty often decrease significantly. Rewards have their place, and used strategically they can be effective to support motivation, especially when combined with the third drive.

PURPOSE DRIVE

The Purpose Drive is your brain's response to fulfilling your unique intrinsic values. This drive seeks to create congruence or alignment between your values and your behaviors. You feel a sense of satisfaction and euphoria when you pursue and fulfill activities that you find meaningful. Your brain responds by releasing the neurochemicals dopamine and oxytocin into your bloodstream, giving you a feeling of pleasure while reinforcing the neural connections related to the behavior. When these connections strengthen, it generates self-directed energy for behaviors that match your goals and pursuits.

The Purpose Drive is thoughtful and uses the executive function of our brain to think through the behaviors, outcomes, and consequences of an action. Before making a decision whether to act, we first evaluate our current situation, environmental support, and the actions we are considering. If we determine there is value in the behavior, a sense of purpose creates energy to act.

An interesting quality of the Purpose Drive is its ability to override the others. This happens when you see great value in doing something that might be painful. The Purpose Drive may determine that enduring pain or discomfort now is worth receiving an outcome that has great meaningfulness later.

An example of this is the student working her way through college to eventually get a better job. This student sees the value of working hard to obtain a degree because it will provide her with better career opportunities and lead to a vocation she is passionate about. In this case, the student is motivated by the valuable outcome.

Another example of the Purpose Drive in action is a person who chooses to become a high-school teacher over a better paying profession. What he values is the internal satisfaction of mentoring and teaching the next generation, rather than the pursuit of wealth.

Daniel Pink, in his book *Drive: The Surprising Truth About What Motivates Us*, makes the case that this drive is the upgraded version of our brain's operating system. He says, "Motivation 3.0, the upgrade we now need, presumes that humans also have a drive to learn, to create, and to better the world."[1]

In the workplace, we can invoke the Purpose Drive in our employees by helping them align work tasks, responsibilities, and outcomes with their values and unique motivators. Of course, this is much easier said than done. And while many leaders will tell you that this is an important element of employee motivation, they often struggle with knowing how to do it.

SURVIVAL   REWARD   PURPOSE

As businesses and organizations flourished throughout the nineteenth and twentieth centuries, most managers relied on motivational tactics that stimulated the Survival Drive. The latter part of the twentieth century saw a significant increase in reward-based motivation as knowledge workers increased and companies competed for the best talent. In today's workplace, most companies still rely on a combination of Survival and Reward to motivate employees. Using these two styles produces some behaviors that leaders want, but it often results in a weakening of self-directed behavior and full engagement. The reliance on these two drives will create higher operational costs due to voluntary turnover, disloyalty, grievances, and lawsuits. By contrast, an organization that successfully leverages the careful use of rewards while also helping employees activate the Purpose Drive in their people can parlay the great potential of human drives into a successful and healthy culture.

BRAIN ANATOMY AND DRIVE

Neuroscience studies have confirmed that the brain has three distinct areas for which each drive is derived. The most primitive part of the brain is the stem and cerebellum. This area is referred to as the **Reptilian Brain,** and it is responsible for both automatic and basic organ function like heartbeat, breathing, digestion, and other fundamental activities that keep you alive. It is also responsible for helping your body manage dangerous situations and threats. In essence, it is mission control for your Survival Drive.

The subcortical area is known as the **Mammalian Brain** and is the next layer above and around the stem and cerebellum. It is responsible for feelings, memories, emotions, and learning. This area seeks to find balance and satisfaction through reward and pleasure. Each reward or feeling of pleasure reinforces neuron connections and leads to more of the same behavior. The mammalian part of your brain guides you to respond to reward and punishment. This part of the brain is the command center for the Reward Drive.

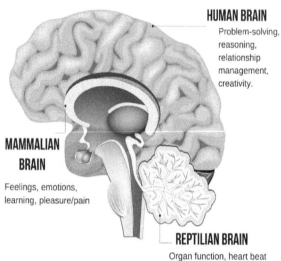

HUMAN BRAIN
Problem-solving, reasoning, relationship management, creativity.

MAMMALIAN BRAIN
Feelings, emotions, learning, pleasure/pain

REPTILIAN BRAIN
Organ function, heart beat breathing, digestion.

The third and final major part of the brain is the Cortex. It is the outer portion and it is known as the **Human Brain** since it is responsible for higher-functioning processes found only in humans and primates. These processing abilities include problem solving, pursuit of goals, reasoning, complex language, relationship management, creativity, and self-regulation. This is where we find the Purpose Drive, which seeks meaning and a sense of significance in our lives.

It's pretty easy to see how leadership styles that rely on survival and reward are relying on the most basic human drives. A style that leverages purpose has the ability to tap into the most powerful part of the brain. This is exactly what Activators do. They use leadership methods and tactics that help people find passion and purpose in their work. In doing so, they help others use more of their brains to pursue meaningful goals.

NEW PERSPECTIVES ON MOTIVATION

As the field of psychology exploded in the mid-twentieth century, psychologists sought to do more than understand human behavior. They wanted to guide and change it. As they looked to understand what makes people tick, motivation became a favored niche for psychological research. Understanding why people behave in certain ways is fascinating, and it provides value in just about every domain of life. The impact of a person's energy is important to education, parenting, religion, science, politics, government, the military, and—perhaps most lucrative of them all—the workplace.

I began my study of motivation and performance in the late 1990s while working on a doctoral degree at the University of Oklahoma. It wasn't long before I felt overwhelmed by all the ideas, concepts, and theories. With my professors' guidance, I plowed ahead. A few years later, I emerged from a forest of courses, books, articles, and papers with a dissertation on motivation and performance. That was nearly two decades ago. Since then, exponentially more data and studies have appeared in this domain. Anyone trying to jump in and understand motivation can easily become confused and frustrated. So let me give you the short version.

Of all the many theories on motivation, a few have become prominent over the past century. Sigmund Freud (1856–1939) put forward one of the most popular and unique theories, positing that motivations are rooted in a person's unconscious sexual desires. Other psychologists proposed their perspectives as well. Alfred Adler (1870–1937) believed that we are motivated by two drives—superiority and power. B. F. Skinner (1904–1990) believed that we couldn't really know a person's motives because they were private. He thought we should not worry about them or seek to understand them. Instead, he proposed the use of reinforcement and punishment tactics to shape behavior in his Operant Conditioning Theory.

Carl Rogers (1902–1987) believed that people are driven by two desires—self-actualization and self-acceptance. William James (1842–1910) created the first list of 37 instinctual desires. He believed instincts developed through natural selection and aided in our survival. Harvard Psychologist William McDougall (1871–1938) expanded James's theory, but used a social perspective. In 1932, he proposed his own set of seventeen instinctual desires.

Abraham Maslow (1908–1970) created one of the most popular motivational theories. He believed motivations could be understood through the progressive fulfillment of basic needs. His "Hierarchy of Needs" may be the most popular theory of motivation ever applied to the workplace. While Maslow provided a basic concept of motivation, his assertion—that lower-level needs must be fulfilled before higher-level needs can be pursued or fulfilled—has been widely rejected for lack of scientific support. His theory reminds us that people have basic needs, which are important to overall well-being, and that those needs impact focus, attention, and behavior.

David McClelland (1917–1998) built on Maslow's work, and proposed the three core motivators of humans—achievement, affiliation, and power. He promoted this theory in his book, *The Achieving Society*, in 1961. He called these "learned needs" because he believed these needs develop through life and experiences.[2]

It's important to understand that during this period it was difficult to gain access to test subjects. Most researchers used college students or animals to test their theories and collect data. It was difficult to find willing adult participants, let alone companies that would allow studies to be conducted within a workplace setting.

Demographic diversity was also hard to find, which raised important questions about how much the study results could be generalized to the population. Most motivation studies in the twentieth century used participants who were primarily Caucasian, middle-class, and located near a university. While these early studies provided some guidance and understanding of people and their motivations, they did little to provide a science-based understanding for what motivates humans to behave in certain ways.

Thankfully, studies in the latter part of the twentieth century have provided much better data for understanding motivation. The broad use of the Internet around the globe has allowed behavioral science to flourish. In addition, powerful software applications have allowed researchers to make big strides toward better measurement and data analysis.

THE EMERGENCE OF BRAIN SCIENCE

Not only do we now have superior behavioral science, we also have insightful data from brain studies to take our understanding to the next level. The field of Neuroscience researches the brain and nervous system for the purpose of understanding and promoting brain health and optimization. Recent technological advances have helped scientists take a giant step forward in understanding the brain. Thanks to the power of electroencephalograms (EEGs) and functional magnetic resonance imaging (fMRI) technology, researchers have discovered and mapped dozens of brain functions and structures. The ability to scan the brain and see patterns in electrical activity and blood flow while certain thoughts and behaviors are happening has provided fascinating insights.

We live in an exciting time where we can leverage this knowledge and apply it to leadership. Coupling the research and insights from both domains create what I call the New Science of Performance.

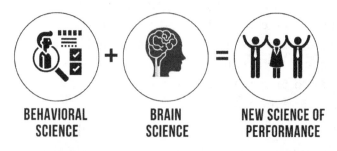

BEHAVIORAL SCIENCE + **BRAIN SCIENCE** = **NEW SCIENCE OF PERFORMANCE**

This new science can help us leverage the most powerful tool we have—our brains. And it's not just about personal growth. Studies are finding that optimized health, thinking, and physiological function occur when our brain is connected to others. This amazing synergy occurs through subconscious communication between people.

This area of research, known as the "social brain," seeks to understand how we thrive when we are in social settings. This area of study holds great promise for anyone who takes the time to learn and apply its powerful insights. This is especially true for leaders. Throughout the rest of this book, I will share many insights and give you practical tactics that will increase your ability to lead and influence more effectively.

PART II

THE NEW SCIENCE OF PERFORMANCE

CHAPTER 3
THE PERFORMANCE PATHWAY

As I ate lunch at a fast-food restaurant in Dallas, I contemplated the best way to help a group of leaders I had been working with that morning. They were frustrated by the attitudes and pervasive apathy they saw in many of their front-line employees. The group opposed every idea I had suggested during the morning session. The company's core problem was how to engage hundreds of highly tenured union employees with a deep disdain for anyone above the management level. I struggled with how to open their minds and move them toward a helpful solution.

Before leaving the restaurant, I asked the young man behind the counter, "Could you refill my cup with water, and if you wouldn't mind, please change out the ice." Nobody wants to have clean water poured into a dirty cup of brown ice, right? The teenager replied enthusiastically, "Sure thing, Sir."

I expected him to dump the ice, refill the cup with new ice, and then top it with water. Instead, he dumped the ice in the sink and turned on the water. Then he rinsed out the cup thoroughly, to make sure it was completely clean. He even gave the water in the cup a couple of swirls to rid the walls of the pesky brown liquid. He continued his mission by refilling the cup with fresh ice and water. Finally, he wiped down the sides of the cup before handing it to me. I said thank you and he responded with a glowing smile, "My pleasure!"

I was so impressed with this young man's service that I asked if I could talk to his manager. He brought his manager over and she asked how she could help me. I told her how well I had been served by the young man. She thanked me and said, "That doesn't surprise me at all, he's always going the extra mile for others."

On the way back to the meeting with my clients, I thought about the experience. I have always had good customer service at this restaurant, but this time it wasn't just good. It was great! I wondered how they can get this level of engagement and performance from ALL of their employees—most of them teenagers.

I decided to tell the group of leaders about my experience as an icebreaker to facilitate our afternoon discussion. After sharing the story, I asked, "If they can get this level of engagement and performance from teenagers in a stressful service job, why is it so difficult for us to do this with the employees here?" A robust and insightful discussion followed for more than an hour. It yielded several key ideas the leaders planned to implement.

That organization's challenge isn't uncommon. As organizations grow, they often shift their focus from people to processes, operational efficiencies, metrics, and other daily tasks that are geared to grow the bottom line. As the complexity of a company increases, caring for the needs of people often takes a back seat. The employee experience disintegrates and people lose trust in those who are higher in the organizational structure. When profits are perceived to be more important than people, employees will instinctively disengage and look for other ways to apply their focus and energy. Sadly, this can reach the point where people apply their motivation to behaviors that undermine the goals of the organization. This is exactly what was happening in the company I was helping.

As we talked through the company's challenges and contrasted it to the fast-food chain's success, the solution became clear. They needed to help each employee clearly understand the company's purpose in a way that shows how their daily work contributes to it. This doesn't happen with a mission or vision statement on a wall. Nor does it occur through a prolific presentation by a chief officer. Rather, it has to be facilitated by a person's direct supervisor. Using the three Activator skills (detailed in chapters 5-7), a leader can use skills of connecting, coaching, and culturing to create the kind of alignment I am referring to.

MOTIVATION'S SECRET SAUCE

We've established that positive, sustainable, and self-directed motivation doesn't come from threats, coercion, or even rewards. We also know that a speech or a great story will not necessarily inspire us to work harder and give our best over an extended period of time. The secret boils down to the alignment between a person's sense of purpose—including what they value and deem meaningful—and the company's mission. This process can only be accomplished when the Purpose Drive is activated.

Neuroscience studies have found that when a person behaves in a purpose-oriented way, the brain stimulates the release of oxytocin—a hormone that acts as a neurotransmitter and is involved in social recognition and bonding.[1] Oxytocin increases feelings of trust and generosity while supporting emotional stability. When people find a sense of meaningfulness in their work, they are also more likely to display higher levels of emotional intelligence, social awareness, and cooperation—facilitating engagement and performance.[2]

Something similar happens with purpose-oriented goals. Several years ago, researchers Edward Deci, Richard Ryan, and Christopher Niemiec from the University of Rochester set out to study how goals impact young adults. They gathered college students who were about to graduate and had them answer questionnaires that documented their career goals. Nearly two years after the students started their jobs, they were asked to answer more questions for the study. The data revealed that students who had started their careers with "purpose goals"—goals that were focused on life improvement, learning, and growth—reported higher levels of satisfaction and well-being. They also had low levels of anxiety and depression.[3]

By contrast, those students who had "profit goals"—goals that were geared towards money and status—reported no increase in levels of satisfaction or well-being since leaving college. Interestingly, these participants were also found to have higher levels of anxiety and depression, even if they had reached their profit goals. This evidence supports the positive impact of goals that are connected to a sense of purpose compared to ones that are extrinsically driven. Purpose-oriented goals can guide us toward deeper meaning in any activity we focus on, including our work.

Our sense of purpose is answered by a question we all ask either consciously or unconsciously–Why? We want to understand why we choose to do something. Purpose drives passion. Our passions aren't derived from incentives; they come from our belief that what we do has a valuable impact. If this connection isn't made, it is just work. Simon Sinek explored this idea in his book, *Start with Why: How Great Leaders Inspire Everyone to*

Take Action. He sums it by saying, "Working hard for something we do not care about is called stress; working hard for something we love is called passion."[4]

Purpose in the workplace are more than general or abstract concepts, like "making a difference" or "changing the world." It isn't even about leaving a legacy, although when you live and work according to your unique purpose you will likely behave in ways that will make a significant impact on others. Keep reading, and I promise to give you a practical way to implement meaning into your own leadership, and help you guide others in gaining this meaningfulness as well.

SELF-DETERMINATION

Two additional contemporary theories of motivation lean heavily on the idea of purpose. Research psychologists, Edward Deci and Richard Ryan of the University of Rochester (co-authors in the goals study previously discussed) and Professor Steven Reiss of Ohio State University, have provided different approaches to understanding people. Applied together, they provide a practical explanation for how we can better lead people. These theories are the most helpful for understanding behavior in the workplace, so much so that I have combined elements of each in the creation of the "Activation" approach. The practical elements of these two theories hold great promise for transforming workplace cultures.

Deci and Ryan's Self-Determination Theory (SDT), explains the inherent growth and motivation tendencies of humans and the conditions that foster them. The most fundamental perspective of this theory is that when three basic human needs are met, optimal motivation levels are supported. The three needs are Autonomy, Competence, and Relatedness. According to Ryan and Deci, each of these needs must be met for a person to feel satisfied and fulfilled.[5]

Daniel Pink uses SDT as the foundational theory in his best-selling book, *Drive: The Surprising Truth About What Motivates Us*.[6] He distilled an exhaustive meta-analysis of motivation literature and SDT to pinpoint the three core needs of Autonomy, Purpose, and Mastery. Susan Fowler uses SDT in her book, *Why Motivating People Doesn't Work and What Does*, to help readers understand how rewards serve as short-lived, "junk food" motivation. She further ties the quality of motivation to the result of individual experiences related to Autonomy, Competence, and Relatedness.[7]

I found SDT to be so helpful that I used it as the theoretical foundation for my doctoral dissertation and several other research studies.[8] Because of its scientific validation and ease of application in the workplace, I have also used this widely accepted theory in my speaking, training, and writing. Over the past two decades, I have expanded the three needs into a model that helps leaders evaluate and take action to strengthen each of the key areas needed for motivation at work. I call it the FRAME model. I will give a detailed explanation in Chapter 5, and in Chapter 8, I'll show you how to apply it to build a healthy and thriving culture.

BASIC DESIRES

While SDT gives us a general perspective of how motivation is hindered or supported, Professor Steven Reiss's *Basic Desires Theory* provides a practical approach for understanding our intrinsic motivators. In contrast to SDT, Basic Desires Theory (BDT) is built on a definitive list of highly practical factors. Reiss and his graduate student Susan M. Havercamp used a large-scale, worldwide exploratory research method conducted over a period of years to formulate a set of sixteen desires, which all people experience at various levels of intensity, that guide energy and behavior.[9] The research suggests that our desire intensity levels (motives) are a manifestation of our deepest values. Based on the research finding, Reiss believed that all motivation is intrinsic in nature and a person's behavior seeks to fulfill one or more of the sixteen basic desires.

BASIC DESIRES - VALUES & MOTIVES

ACCEPTANCE	FAMILY	ORDER	SOCIAL CONTACT
BEAUTY	HONOR	PHYSICAL ACTIVITY	STATUS
CURIOSITY	IDEALISM	POWER	TRANQUILITY
EATING	INDEPENDENCE	SAVING	VENGEANCE

Reiss's research discovered several insightful principles of motivation. Here are a few:

✦ Desires are a combination of our intrinsic needs and values.

✦ The intensity of our desires drives our behavior and defines our personality.

✦ Interpersonal conflicts are often found between people who have opposing viewpoints (intensity of values) on a particular desire. For instance, one person has a weak desire for power, while another has a strong desire for it.

✦ We can predict people's behaviors by their strong and weak desires.

✦ Your desires make your life worth living.

✦ All behaviors and pursuits are attempts to fulfill our desires (values).

⚡ Desires can compete for priority. This is often what causes conflicts in our heads and makes it tough to decide which activities to prioritize. For example, do you accept a new job with more responsibility and influence (desire for power), or do you focus on parenting responsibilities (desire for family)?

You can use the insights of BDT to better understand yourself as well as the values and motivations of the people you lead. As a leader, this insight will help you to engage your employees by placing them in roles and situations where their motivators align with the company needs. Understanding basic desires allows you to have robust coaching conversations where you help employees understand their intrinsic motivators and better lead themselves. We will dive deeper into BDT in Chapters 5 and 6, where I show you exactly how to use this method to understand the deepest motivations of others.

LEADING HIGH PERFORMANCE

Many leaders make the same mistake I did when I assumed that a person was engaged if they exhibit motivated behaviors. When you see motivated behavior at work, it's easy to believe that an employee is engaged. But this isn't always the case.

Consider Cal, who was an employee of mine several years ago. He was a likable young man who always completed his assignments quickly. Like most high achievers, he started his day focused on a list of tasks. That said, he also arrived at work later than most of his peers. I let that slide since he always got the job done on time, if not early.

Cal enjoyed social interaction with his colleagues but didn't allow himself to indulge in it until after he completed his tasks and attended to a host of daily email requests. He took short lunch breaks and often ate a homemade sandwich at his desk as he continued to work. His peers seemed to like him and, based on his output and behavior, any manager would have loved to have him on their team.

Cal appeared to be the ideal employee, and for the first several months of supervising him, I thought the same. His deadlines had some scheduled flexibility, so I didn't see it as a problem if he came in later than his peers did, since it wasn't past 9 a.m. But then I began to notice him leaving the office, for an hour or two, a couple of times per week. When I asked him about it, he gave me some plausible reasons; a doctor's appointment, taking a late lunch, running home to grab something — things that didn't really merit a reprimand. However, it prompted me to keep a closer watch on him.

Over time, I saw more concerning behaviors. There were times when his work quality looked rushed. For a while, I assumed his lack of thoroughness was due to youth and the need for continual development. I took the time to coach him. He was receptive, listened well, and appeared to want to grow and develop.

A little while later, two of my employees requested a confidential meeting. They had concerns about Cal and his lack of support for the team's collaborative efforts. One came forward saying, "When we invite him to join us for a team lunch or a break, he declines. It's like he's a different person in the afternoon."

From then on, I paid closer attention to Cal's behavior each afternoon. What I discovered shocked me. During the afternoon, Cal's focus wasn't entirely on his job duties. He was using his phone, emails, and Internet to manage a side business — one he'd launched more than a year earlier.

I was perplexed and asked myself, "Why I didn't see this behavior sooner?" I confronted him about the situation, and we ultimately came up with a plan to help him transition from his work to running his own business. Prior to this situation, I had written a dissertation on motivation and performance in the workplace, so I was curious as to why I had failed to see the red flags until so late.

In one conversation I'd had with him, I asked for some feedback. "Cal, at face value, you seemed very motivated and engaged in your work here. I thought you really liked what you were doing. In hindsight, however, I see that you weren't engaged even though you got your work done. Is there something more I could have done to have led you better or engaged you?"

He responded with, "I am! I think I'm more motivated to achieve than anyone on the team. But my goal is to run my own business." His point was clear and served as a great reminder to me of the difference between motivation and engagement. A person's internal energy to pursue a basic desire is raw and rudimentary, but that doesn't guarantee that they'll be fully engaged in the task. Engagement at work occurs when a person applies their commitment, and discretionary effort toward team and organizational goals. This is where misalignment occurred for Cal. Perhaps I could have done a better job of helping him align his desires and goals with the organization's purpose. But even if I would have done that well, his personal desire to run his own business may still have been more meaningful to him than working for a corporation.

In this situation, Cal had two support mechanisms for his motivation and energy. Our ability to move from motivation to engagement (committed and guided application of energy) is going to be hindered or supported by our environment, which includes people, processes, culture, and resources. Optimizing motivation and converting it to engaged behaviors is contingent on the environment. This is where the contrasting scientific perspectives of BDT and SDT provide us with a broader understanding of how the two mechanisms work together. While BDT is focused on internal factors that drive motivation, SDT explains the external factors that either support or hinder engagement.

Together, these mechanisms act as support system scaffolding that encourages engagement. When a high level of internal energy (motivation) is being created and is concurrently supported by external factors, a person's potential to become fully engaged skyrockets. This is where the magic happens.

Remember back to a time when you had an idea, one that you believed to be brilliant. What happened when you shared it with someone, and they shot it down? You likely walked away feeling deflated. You had a high level of motivation (psychological energy), but when you were placed in an environment that was negative rather than supportive, it resulted in a distinct reduction of motivation. Unfortunately, this is what often happens in the workplace. Most employees want to be a part of something great, they want to love their job, they want to find purpose and meaningfulness in what they do, and they want to thrive in the place where they spend a third of their lives. However, many teams and organizational environments hinder a person's optimal motivation and, ultimately, their engagement level.

So how do we supercharge high performance? Workplace studies show that a person's intelligence, skill, knowledge, and experience are determining factors that influence performance. They are like the major parts of a car's engine. They must be working at a sufficient level to do the job well. This book won't focus on these elements. Instead, it will focus on the factors that can create a turbocharging effect like motivation, leadership, and the environment. While motivation is like the fuel for an engine, the elements of leadership (fire), and the environment (oxygen) work together to increase capacity and capability (horsepower). When these are combined at the right levels, the result is powerful.

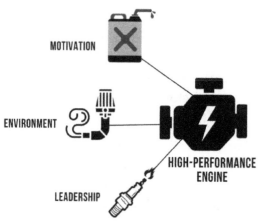

A leader who facilitates this process becomes a catalyst for positive energy. Activation is a unique employee-leader interaction that supports the alignment of internal motivation and external environment with daily work. Rooted in the scientific principles of Basic Desires Theory and Self-Determination Theory, the Activation process tells us how to flip a person's engagement switch to the "ON" position. When you learn how to harness both the internal and external, you create a cycle of energy that boosts engagement and leads to greater achievement and higher performance.

Are you ready to be an Activator? Do you want to help people optimize their motivation and transform their lives? If so, buckle up and keep reading. You are about to learn how to become a leader who unleashes people from what holds them back and launches them toward their potential.

CHAPTER 4
LIGHTING-UP THE BRAIN

Now that you have a good understanding of how motivation and engagement work together to create high performance, let's get a practical understanding of how the Activation approach works.

In the previous chapter, I used an analogy of a leader being the spark plug within a high-performance engine. Effective leaders function as a spark that ignites all the other parts of the engine. If you have ever had a car with a misfiring spark plug, you know what happens. The engine coughs and skips—it doesn't work well. An effective spark plug is a critical component for the function, power, and coordination of the entire engine. A leader's interaction with their people works in much the same way, creating that spark of energy, which helps to determine the power of each person and the level of coordination on their team.

A few years ago, I met with my supervisor to share a big idea. After running him through my strategy for the upcoming year, along with the project plan and budget, I awaited his response. The plan was audacious. One portion of it called for the execution of more than one hundred executive-level training seminars across eight cities, including London, Hong Kong, and São Paulo—all to be administered by a team of six people. On one hand, I was proud of the plan my team had created. It showed how we could serve more than six thousand leaders around the world. On the other, I was nervous that he'd think we were being too ambitious and wouldn't trust me to move forward.

He asked a few clarifying questions, and then paused for a moment, looking over the spreadsheet of cities and seminar offerings. Then he looked at me and asked, "How confident are you that you can execute this with your small team?"

With as much confidence as I could muster, I looked him in the eyes and said, "One-Hundred percent!"

In all honesty, I had doubts. It was an ambitious goal with many opportunities for failures. The morning before, I had asked myself why I was willing to go out on a limb like this. I reminded myself that my performance evaluation scores were dependent on my achievement level. Even if I reduced the goal by 25%, I would still have created a challenging and high-impact objective for the company. But I knew my team could do it. It was a risk I was willing to take because I had a passion for what we were doing.

After hearing the determination in my voice, he smiled and said, "I have full confidence in you. You are a pro." The way he said it lit me up. He could have said, "Okay, good luck," or "This is going to be tough, so I'll let you move ahead." Instead, he chose words that were empowering and supportive. His words activated my energy, not just my confidence to achieve the goal and to reach it prolifically. He was an Activator.

When we activate something, we turn it on. I like to think about activation as igniting or unleashing something that has been dormant. Like an ember that burns small and silent. When stoked or prodded, it burst into a flame. And just like that smoldering ember, a person can be invigorated by the elements that surround them.

We all need an Activator to stoke our potential and facilitate the discovery of our values, purpose, and passion. Too many people lack that fire of passion and motivation because their flame hasn't been nurtured. It hasn't received the oxygen it needs to grow and thrive, and it hasn't been given a spark. But once we're activated, we feel alive.

This is because activation produces an optimal brain state where the neurotransmitters—dopamine and serotonin—along with the hormone oxytocin, stimulate better feeling, thinking and processing. Activated people are smarter, faster, and stronger. They are more competent, confident, and resilient.

The idea of activation is rooted in the belief that we all have the capacity to be better with the help of others. Anyone who wants to become an Activator must commit to relaxing their need to compete and win against colleagues or employees. Activators view success differently. Rather than it being a state of individual achievement, it's a viewpoint that success is created when we win together. This is the opposite of what most of us have learned throughout our lives.

Children are taught, at an early age, to compete to win in all aspects of life. Individualism and independence are taught, while interdependence and collaboration are often punished. On the sports field, our children learn to beat each other. Even though players are taught to work as a team, pass the ball, and help teammates. Inevitably, only one or two people get the spotlight and praised as the MVP.

We compete for ranking in our graduation class, we compete for jobs, and we compete for bonuses and raises. Our default is to prioritize winning, beat others down, and achieve a position of superiority. Our world becomes a difficult place when we see everything through a lens of winning or losing. This is especially true in the workplace.

Activators understand that nobody can come close to reaching their potential and becoming the best they can be on their own. Activators look for the greatness in people and find ways to unearth their strengths and potential contributions. An old African proverb says, "If you want to go fast, go by yourself. If you want to go far, go together." In a world where we are enticed by achieving things quickly, we easily lose sight of the value of far. This is similar to the difference between something made cheap and something made with quality. Your life and the lives of others, along with what you and others can accomplish, are far too important to focus on getting anywhere fast and cheap. You deserve quality.

Activators use a team perspective by viewing each member as a critical piece of a puzzle—a perspective in which the final product is dependent on every piece working together. The Activator's job is to help each piece find its place, to position them to contribute in their unique way.

It's important to remember that in a team setting, the formal leaders are not the only people who can activate others. Anyone can play this role if they are committed to helping others succeed. In fact, high-performing teams don't just have a good leader, the individuals all actively help each other to achieve and succeed. We all need people around who help us and who have strengths in areas we don't. We need people who enjoy the tasks we dislike. This is another reason why we want to do

46

everything possible to activate people around us—employees, peers, and even those above us.

Imagine a few thousand years ago when our ancestors were hunters and gatherers. What would happen if they competed against one another while they were hunting for food? The tribes that worked together, where members helped each other, were the ones that ultimately succeeded. These tribes and their members thrived because they worked together in all aspects of their lives, especially when fighting wild animals, defending their territory, hunting for food, and raising children.

The Activation approach takes us back to the root of who we are as humans. Our brains have been wired to help and support the achievement of people around us, knowing that this approach is what ultimately leads to success and well-being for all. A primitive need to help others is woven into our DNA. When we do this, it creates a deeper sense of satisfaction and meaningfulness that keeps us thriving as human beings.

Think back, have you ever altruistically offered assistance with a work problem, gave money to a homeless person, or offered your time to someone who needed it. How did you feel after you did that? Did you have a sense of satisfaction or happiness when you saw the impact of your actions? There is a reason you felt that way. It is because, for a moment, you tapped into the core of how your brain works.

When we are activated, our brain is stimulated in a special way. Activation leverages our motivation, and it expands our brain capacity. It shifts our primary mode from "survive" to "thrive," allowing us to leverage our full capability.

THE NEUROSCIENCE OF LEADERSHIP

The word "Activation" describes the awakening of our psychological energy and accurately illustrates what is happening inside our brains. Activation implies that something is being "turned on" in the brain and nervous system. Research conducted by Richard Boyatzis and Anthony Jack looked at fMRI scans to study brain function and the impact of differing manager-employee interactions. When employees were asked to recall experiences with managers who listened well, showed empathy, and asked about personal goals and dreams, fourteen regions of the employee's brains were activated. The activation was marked by a significant increase in neuron activity. When employees were asked to recall experiences with managers who displayed controlling and demanding behaviors during the interactions, only six regions of the brain were activated. Even worse, eleven regions of the brain were deactivated.[1]

This means leaders, who use the right approach, can literally "light up" the brains of the people they lead! Positive and supportive interactions between the leader and employee activate multiple regions of the brain, resulting in an increase to motivation, energy, and visioning; better cognitive processing, creativity, and focus; as well as favorable hormone production.

Think about a time when you were highly motivated to do something after a conversation with a boss, friend, or colleague. When we have collaborative conversations—where we feel safe, empowered, and inspired—our brains become activated, our confidence surges and creativity increases. Moreover, levels of dopamine and oxytocin spike, which boosts feelings of empowerment, positivity, trust, and confidence.

Activation is an approach to leadership that requires interdisciplinary thinking in order to integrate key knowledge from the fields of behavioral science and neuroscience. In fact, the Activator perspective can be considered an Interpersonal Neurobiology (IPNB) approach to leadership due to its interconnection of brain biology and social function. By leveraging principles gleaned from these fields, we can optimize the brain function and behavior of people, helping them to become happier and more successful in every part of their lives.

While I don't expect you to become an expert in brain science, it does help to know a little about how the different parts of the brain work. The information in the next few pages will help you on your journey to becoming an Activator for the people you lead.

BRAIN SCIENCE BASICS

Your brain is more powerful than any technology, device, or computer that has ever been created. It is indeed your greatest asset. How you manage and use your brain is a large determining factor for your relationships, health, career, happiness, and success. Your brain has the capability to process complex information faster than can be calculated by any man-made machine. For instance, think about how fast you take in a statement that a person makes to you. Within a fraction of a second, you're able to listen, process the words to create understanding, give context to other information, interpret and give meaning to that information, decide if the message is positive or threatening, decide how to respond, and take action. You are amazing!

The average brain generates tens of thousands of thoughts per day. It has more than 100 billion neurons—cells that communicate through electrical-chemical connections. Your brain has thousands of neural-networks connecting the neurons you have created through thinking, learning, and experiencing life.

It is Mission Control for your entire body, managing all your functions, including the activities that you don't need to think about—like maintaining your heartbeat and breathing. In fact, you are mostly unaware of the thousands of tasks that your brain initiates and processes each day. They happen automatically and subconsciously.

The brain is not only the most intricate and powerful organ in the human body; it's also the most complex object we know. This is part of what fascinates scientists and practitioners who study it. There is so much we don't know. But what scientists have learned so far provides many practical insights into how we can become better people—if we take the time to learn how to leverage its power. I introduced you to the three parts of the brain (Reptilian, Mammalian, and Human) in Chapter 2. Now let's take a deeper look at the different parts of your brain, and how they work together.

BRAIN STEM AND CEREBELLUM

The brain stem is located at the base of the brain and is connected to the spinal cord. This is the area we have previously identified as the "Reptilian Brain." It regulates signals between the brain and the spinal cord. The cerebellum is located just behind the brain stem and controls the coordination and timing of your movements, as well as many of our automatic reactions to stimulus. This part of the brain is found deep inside your head and is the most delicate portion of the brain.

LIMBIC SYSTEM

The second section is the limbic system, which is located just above and outside the brain stem. Known as the "Mammalian

Brain," it is composed of several important sub-structures, including:

Thalamus: The traffic guide that sends and receives sensory information to other parts of the brain.

Amygdala: One of the processing units for emotion and memory.

Hippocampus: Aids memory processing and connection throughout the brain.

Hypothalamus: Controls hormone functions that are related to feelings of thirst, hunger, and fatigue. It also regulates your body temperature.

Nucleus Accumbens: The reward center of your brain that controls the release of the bonding and trust hormone oxytocin, as well as the neurochemical dopamine that reinforces connections in the brain and gives people a feeling of satisfaction and well-being.

CORTEX

The Cortex also referred to as the Cerebral Cortex and the "Human Brain" is the outer layer of the brain and is responsible for our higher-level thinking and behavior. The cerebral cortex is divided into four areas.

Frontal Lobe: Neuroscientists acknowledge this section to be the part of the brain that makes us uniquely human. It is responsible for our behaviors of thinking, processing, making meaning, managing emotions, and making choices.

Temporal Lobe: Found around the sides of the brain. It aids abstract thinking, complex processing, problem solving, understanding of metaphors, and use of language.

Parietal Lobe: This area is located at the top of the brain and is responsible for receiving and processing sensory information such as taste, hearing, smell, and touch.

Occipital Lobe: Found in the back and lower part of the brain, it is responsible for visual processing. It aids mapping visual input and cues, reading, and interpretation of object movement.

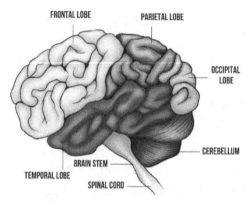

This book isn't intended to be an anatomy class, but it is helpful for you to understand the interconnected elements and how they work. As amazing as it is, it's also obvious that the brain can have problems. Brain problems can hinder a person's motivation, engagement, and performance. Problems include:

Despondence: Our brain will function sub-optimally during emotional and psychological challenges. This occurs for various reasons, including chemical imbalances, poor diet, genetic factors, and physical health. Despondence manifests in many ways, such as depression, anxiety, obsessions or compulsions, apathy, and mental lethargy.

Damage: Brains can be damaged in many ways. Head trauma and chemical dependency are two of the most common ways human brains are damaged. Damage can also occur from malnutrition and disease.

Disease: Diseases such as dementia and Alzheimer's are the best-known brain degenerative diseases. Brain cancer is also a major problem that hinders proper brain function. A disease that strikes other parts of the body, like muscular dystrophy, can also have a damaging effect on the brain, as can the treatment of the disease.

Decline: Decline occurs when the brain loses processing speed and accuracy. Studies show that for most people, their brain begins to decline when they retire from daily work. This is usually because they are not as mentally challenged in retirement as they were at work. The brain works like a muscle: If you don't use it, you lose it.

Deactivation: Deactivation occurs when the brain is not using all of its parts in unison to create optimal function and health. Some areas of the brain literally shut down during deactivation. This often occurs as a result of feelings of fear, stress, boredom, or emotional distress.

The exciting news is that your brain isn't fixed or static. Neuroscience studies show that you can grow it and build it. You can make it stronger, faster, and more powerful, even if you have suffered any of the 5 Ds. This is because your brain has what researchers call neuroplasticity—the ability to heal, grow, and change, throughout your life.

Activators lead with the brain in mind by seeking ways to optimize the brains of their people. Activators take action to create brain-friendly, growth-promoting environments where everyone can thrive. They know that they have the power to light up someone's brain in a way that unleashes them to be their best in every part of their life. Activators find great meaning in helping others live up to their potential. So, how do you become an Activator? That's the subject of the next chapter.

CHAPTER 5
BECOMING AN ACTIVATOR

Now that you understand the concept of activation, it's time to learn how to become a leader who applies these principles to your everyday work. Activation is more than a leadership theory: it is an action-based approach that requires focus and effort. A person who sets out to be an Activator is one who puts thought and effort into unleashing people from the things holding them back and empowering them to take their lives to the next level.

Let me make this crystal clear by giving you an example of what Activators *don't* do. You have probably endured the not so delightful experience of buying a vehicle from a dealership. A few years ago, I wanted to buy a specific make and model of car that I had been thinking about for a while. My excitement increased as I continued to window shop online. I did my homework and learned everything I could about the car, including the extra features and pricing. Then on a Friday afternoon, with feelings of anticipation and excitement, I made the drive to the dealership, ready to buy, but I also felt apprehensive and unsure of how the deal would go down. I had the financial means to buy, but I didn't want to pay more than necessary.

After parking my car in the dealership's parking lot, I got out of my car and began looking at a row of cars that were similar to the one I wanted to buy. It didn't take long before two gentlemen appeared from two separate doors of the building nearby. Each was determined to reach me before the other. They looked like they were competing in a power-walking race until one of the men became aware of how ridiculous they looked and decided to peel off his route and head back to the building.

When the man drew near, he stuck out his hand and said, "Hi, I'm Bob!" Smiling, I shook his hand and told him my name. It didn't take long before he began using antiquated, poorly executed sales techniques. He asked the same questions I'd heard many times before when shopping for a car. "What kind of payment range are you looking to stay within? Are you wanting to finance?" Then he looked to my vehicle. "I see your car over there. Those have great trade-in value. Will you be trading it?" I began to feel annoyed.

I told him I wanted to know the price of the vehicle since it had more options than what I had looked at online. I wasn't concerned with paying more to get a few options that I wanted. He pulled a notebook from his back pocket and searched it for a few seconds before finally saying, "I'll have to go in and get the price. I'll get the keys as well and we can take it for a spin."

I expected him to return within a couple of minutes; instead, he was gone for fifteen. I stood in the parking lot growing tired and frustrated. When he finally emerged from the shiny glass building, he waved a key fob. "Hey, I got the keys." He approached and tossed them to me. "Let's go for a ride!"

I caught them and replied, "Thank you, but did you get the price?"

He stumbled on his response but seemed proud of his recovery when he admitted, "Well, I didn't, but once we finish the test drive let's go back to my office and we will talk numbers." I rolled my eyes as I sat down in the driver's seat.

The badgering didn't stop on the drive. The salesman obviously wanted to assess my ability to afford the vehicle. I felt interrogated as he hurled question after question about my job, my education, and my family. He even wanted to know what I was planning to do Saturday night! I hadn't been asked that many questions since my last doctor's visit.

By the time we pulled back into the parking lot, I was fatigued by the experience. Outside the car once more, I handed him the key fob as he extended the invitation, "How about we go inside and talk about getting you into this baby!"

Part of me wanted to move forward, but most of me wanted to leave. I said, "Bob, thank you for your time. But I'm going to keep looking." I made my way through the maze of cars, returning to my own vehicle, feeling disappointed. Badgering Bob watched me as I drove toward the exit. The poor man looked defeated and confused, so I gave him a friendly wave goodbye.

I too felt deflated. I knew the car-buying process wouldn't be a Disney World experience, but I didn't expect to leave feeling so demotivated. I had been primed and was ready to buy that day, but the salesman had depleted all my energy. All Bob had to do was cultivate and support an environment that would take me to the next natural step of the process.

This is exactly how millions of people experience their work each day. They have motivation and energy within them, but their environment stands in the way of them becoming truly engaged. Your employees want to be a part of something worthwhile. They want to do more than just work a job. They want to love their work.

The goal of any leader should be to lead in a way that supports a person's internal motivation while also creating an external environment that encourages full engagement. To make that happen, leaders must understand and take action to strengthen two important mechanisms.

Activation occurs when two complementary motivation mechanisms—the internal and the external—work together to support each other. These mechanisms are not just types of motivation like extrinsic or intrinsic. Rather, they are the *origin* of the forces that create your energy.

The Internal mechanism is the force that is internal, while external mechanisms originate outside of you. Motivation is optimized and engagement is encouraged when we build strength in each mechanism and facilitate a synergy between the two. When one mechanism is weak, a person's motivation is diminished and engagement is discouraged.

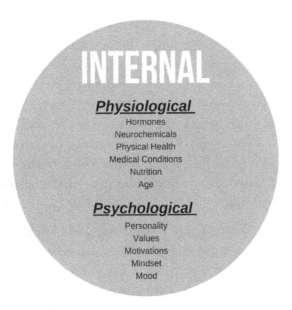

THE INTERNAL MECHANISM OF MOTIVATION

The internal motivation mechanism is made up of your physiology and your psychology. Physiology includes hormone levels, neurochemical makeup, health, organ function, medical condition, age, medications, circulation, nutrition, and even the level of a person's physical movement during the day. Believe it or not, how you are sitting right now impacts your motivation. Your posture can affect your blood circulation, hormone levels, energy, and your brain function.

I have coached several executive leaders who have confided in me that they don't have the level of energy, stamina, and motivation they once had. In fact, this is a concerning situation for many business leaders who have achieved their current status through their drive and intellect. It is not uncommon to find a cognitive decline alongside a loss of motivation in people as they age. This is why the first thing I recommend when coaching a leader who is struggling with their motivation and energy is to visit their primary care physician for a complete physical and blood panel analysis. It is important for both men and women because health and hormone levels such as testosterone and thyroxine can have a significant impact on your energy. We all know that the things that get maintained perform better and last longer than the things that don't. This principle applies to the car you drive and the tools you use—and it also applies to our body and brain.

If you are interested in optimizing your motivation, I suggest you eat for healthy energy; that means more vegetables and healthy proteins, low-glycemic carbs, and eliminate as much sugar as possible. Sugars and high-glycemic foods are like slot machines at a casino. They pay out a short-term energy boost to keep you coming back, but over the long term, they rob you of your energy.

Movement and exercise are also key factors for your energy level. During the day, it is important to allow your blood to circulate and to maintain hormone balance. Human bodies weren't meant to sit all day. Simply taking a break every 45 to 60 minutes for a short walk or stretch can have a significant impact on your motivation.

The second major factor of your internal motivation mechanism is your psychology. When people think about psychology, they often think of something deeply rooted in their unconscious minds. This may be so, but I'm referring to things you already know or can know about yourself, like your personality, values, motivations, and needs.

The clearer you are with each of these elements, the more control you have over your behavior and your happiness. This is why taking the time to understand yourself is important. And from a leadership perspective, this is why it's so important that we help our followers gain personal awareness and self-insight. In doing so, they will become more self-directed in their behaviors, often resulting in greater motivation, engagement, and satisfaction in their work and in their lives.

BUILDING INTERNAL STRENGTH

The most powerful way to strengthen your internal motivation mechanism is to have a deep understanding of your Basic Desires (Chapter 3). The sixteen scientifically derived desires, discovered by Professor Reiss, can help us to understand what drives us intrinsically and serves as our most powerful motivators. Knowing yourself well means that you have taken time and effort to think deeply about what has value, is important, and fulfills you. One of the great keys to life satisfaction and a sense of happiness is having a good understanding of what energizes you and what makes your life worth living.

As leaders, we must see each employee as an individual with a set of desires that are a result of their genetic makeup, personality, and life experiences. This is where supporting motivation can get tricky. Reiss's list of desires provides us insight into what people are really pursuing through their behavior, even at work. It turns out that the sixteen motivators are an amalgamation of our needs, values, and aspirations and are intertwined into every element of our lives.

Activators listen, inquire, and get to know their direct reports so they can understand their motivators. Then they help each employee align their desires with their work. This alignment boosts intrinsic motivation, which provides sustained motivation and self-directed action. When employees gain insights into their desires, it helps them clarify their purpose and understand which activities are most meaningful to them.

I'll share how you can help employees gain this insight and strengthen their internal motivation mechanism in Chapter 6. You can also read an explanation of each desire in Appendix A. For now, let's take a quick look at how Reiss defines each desire in his book, *The Reiss Motivation Profile: What Motivates You?*.[1]

It's important to remember that you have a level of intensity for each of these factors that can affect how much it will motivate you. If you have an average or moderate intensity level for a desire, it will only motivate you sometimes. Factors for which you have a strong level of intensity will lead you to take action to fulfill that desire. A weak or low intensity level will lead you to take action away from the desire.

Acceptance: The desire for positive self-regard.

Beauty: The desire for aesthetically appealing experiences.

Curiosity: The desire for understanding.

Eating: The desire to consume food.

Family: The desire to raise children and spend time with siblings.

Honor: The desire for upright character.

Idealism: The desire for social justice.

Independence: The desire for self-reliance.

Order: The desire for structure and stability.

Physical Activity: The desire for muscle exercise.

Power: The desire for influence of will.

Saving: The desire to collect things.

Social Contact: The desire for companionship with peers.

Status: The desire for respect based on social standing.

Tranquility: The desire to avoid experiencing anxiety and pain.

Vengeance: The desire to confront those who frustrate or offend us.

THE EXTERNAL MECHANISM OF MOTIVATION

The external motivation mechanism is made up of environmental influences. Remember how you felt when your thought or idea was rejected, laughed at, or was shot down by someone? Those are examples of times when the external motivation mechanism impacted your motivation and willingness to engage. This phenomenon is so common that we have several popular expressions in the English language to explain this loss of motivation. "I got shot down. They burst my bubble. He took the wind out of my sail. I feel deflated." When we say those, we are expressing that feeling of a lack of environmental support and the associated loss of energy and motivation.

A person's environment is extremely powerful, and it is made up of many factors, including cultural expectations, religious standards, and familial norms. Your environment also includes how people communicate with you, how they accept you, your level of autonomy, and how your leader interacts with you. An unsupportive environment can have a significant impact on your motivation, as it can literally cause your brain to shut down important functions.

This is why the external mechanism is so important. It can support or hinder your ability to overcome obstacles, navigate difficulties, and conquer self-doubt. You can do more and be more when your environment is supportive. Numerous studies have shown the positive impact a supportive group of colleagues or friends has on a person's determination and resilience.

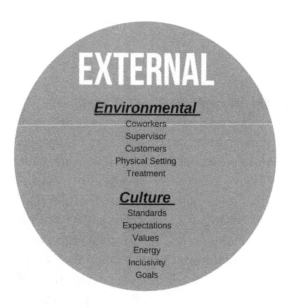

BUILDING EXTERNAL STRENGTH

Think about the various groups, associations, and friendship circles you've been involved with throughout your life. The ones that held your deepest loyalty, and that you were most engaged with, were likely groups that had a unique set of characteristics—highly supportive of your values, ideas, and goals. They probably challenged you, in a positive way, to do better and to become a better person.

These kinds of groups are attractive because they are composed of people who have similar goals, and the members have created a sense of trust and camaraderie. The group interaction boosts your energy and confidence in a way that motivates you to engage and support others. When these types of groups form, they often grow in numbers because people want this powerfully beneficial social interaction. The people involved in these groups often take great pride in what they do together, so much so, that they can't help but to tell other people about it.

Two decades ago, I was invited to join a breakfast club. We met every Friday at 6:30 a.m., to drink coffee and talk about life, work, business, family, faith, sports, and just about anything else that was on our minds. As a person who doesn't particularly like waking up at 5:30 a.m., I wasn't too keen on 6:30 meetings every Friday, but I wanted to check it out.

After only two meetings, I found that I enjoyed it so much that I made a commitment to attend every Friday. This group of men became some of my best friends and closest confidants. After a few years, the group had grown so large it was time to start a new coffee group, so that more people could benefit from its support and camaraderie. I attended this one for four more years until I moved to a different state.

Many men became a part of these early morning coffee meetings over the years. Some stuck with the same group for years, while others started or attended other coffee groups around town. As I write this book, the original coffee group has been running strong for more than 20 years! Why? Because the members get so much out of it. They leave each meeting feeling activated.

The people who surround us have an immense impact on our motivation and willingness to engage. The role of a leader can't be understated in a group like this. In fact, leaders of successful teams don't just create and communicate the purpose and vision of the team, they facilitate an environment where people feel a sense of ownership and take action to contribute in positive ways.

Workplace environments where people are authentically valued and invested in the group's well-being create ownership and engagement that we all desire. Using the FRAME model is an evidence-based approach that can help you do this.

FRAME THE ENVIRONMENT

Five factors contribute to environments that supercharge motivation and encourage engagement. The five factors make up the acronym FRAME. A great way to remember this model is to think of it as a "FRAMEwork" — a FRAME model for work.

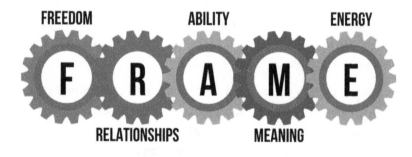

FREEDOM

In a speech to the Virginia Commonwealth on March 23, 1775, Patrick Henry demanded, "Give me liberty, or give me death!" His convictions, shared by many, led the fight for freedom and ultimately the formation of the United States of America. Freedom is the central value of every human, and many believe it to be a fundamental human right. Research has shown that it is also a fundamental pathway for motivation. A person must feel a sense of freedom and autonomy in their work to engage in the activity with full effort. If we feel we are being forced to do something, we respond with an innate reaction of rebellion.

Leaders can help create freedom in the work environment by involving employees in the goal-setting process, or allowing employees to provide input and self-direction regarding how the goals are met. Creating the right environment requires that you lead with trust and seek to empower people to take initiative and make choices that direct their actions and outcomes. In an environment of freedom, people are:

- Given control of how they get their work done.

- Involved in making key decisions that affect the team and even the company.

- Encouraged to be innovative and generate new ideas and processes in their work.

- Inspired to develop themselves for their current and future job roles.

- Viewed as partners and colleagues.

RELATIONSHIPS

Deci and Ryan's research on motivation supports the fundamental principle that people thrive within healthy relationships—when they have good connections with others. Our connections with other people have been a point of interest to psychologists for decades. Multitudes of studies confirm the fundamental need humans have for relationships. Work relationships have the power to support or hinder your natural motivation and desire to give your best effort. In an environment where leaders cultivate healthy relationships and strong connections between people, trust, and camaraderie grow.

ABILITY

Think about an activity you perform poorly. Do you look forward to participating in that activity? Of course not. Nobody wants to experience failure over and over again. If you do not think you will successfully complete a task, activity, or assignment, you will not want to engage in it. Leaders help employees build a sense of competence by creating goals that are challenging enough to stretch the person, but without overextending them and creating a feeling of being overwhelmed. Effective leaders also look for ways to place employees into roles that align with their strengths.

MEANING

Nothing lights the fire of motivation like participating in an activity that is aligned with our deepest values. When a person becomes fully aware of their intrinsic values, they gravitate toward activities that are meaningful and fulfilling. Many books declare the importance of meaning at work to motivate and engage people. Unfortunately, they don't tell you how to make this happen.

Most people don't understand how people define "meaning" in their life, much less in the workplace. Some say it has to do with finding something altruistic in work, while others believe it comes from having a significant impact—by "changing the world" in some way. Not only is this oversimplified, but it can also frustrate people who are overwhelmed with life responsibilities and trying to manage each day effectively.

People find meaning in work on two levels. On an individual level, a person finds meaning when they can align their basic desires with their work tasks, goals, and team mission. The second level is achieved when a team or group of coworkers create meaning together. This becomes a powerful catalyst for high performance.

ENERGY

The energy within an environment is fundamentally emotional. Each person within a given setting contributes emotional energy. These individual contributions merge to create greater environmental energy that has a major impact on how people feel, think, behave, and interact with each other.

I'm sure you have had the experience of being in the presence of someone who is an "energy vampire." This person seems to suck the energy out of everyone around them. This kind of person is usually a chronic complainer or pessimist. They view most things negatively and act as if they have no control on the events in their life. They are not happy and actively seek to recruit people into their clan of energy zappers. The old saying, "misery loves company" rings true with these people.

By contrast, Activators serve as tone-setters for the people around them, promoting positive energy in the workplace. They also identify negative energy inputs and take action to neutralize them. Emotional energy is crucial for any environment and serves to shape the culture.

You can use the FRAMEwork model to assess your current environment to determine where you have strengths and weaknesses. That analysis will then help you decide which elements need attention and strengthening. You can also use the FRAME-work model to think through how you will communicate with people. I call this "FRAMEing" your communication. In doing so, you ensure that your communication, whether verbal or written, addresses the broad needs people have during the communication process.

Ask yourself these questions.

- ⚡ Am I communicating a sense of freedom and autonomy? Have I facilitated a sense of choice? (Freedom)

- ⚡ Am I connecting the information in the communication to people, a sense of mutual care, and supportive relationships? (Relationships)

- ⚡ Will people feel they can succeed? Am I providing adequate resources? (Ability)

- ⚡ Can the person align this to their intrinsic values (motivators)? How? (Meaning)

- ⚡ Is the energy of the communication — words, phrases, connotations — positive? Am I facilitating a sense of pride? (Energy)

Later in the book, I will discuss specific brain-friendly tactics you can use to create environments that engage your people.

BECOMING AN ACTIVATOR

The process of activating people is a cycle in which the internal and external motivational mechanisms support each other. The Activator's role is not only to help a person strengthen both motivation mechanisms but also to facilitate a continual supportive cycle. That cycle comes to life when one mechanism gives energy to the other.

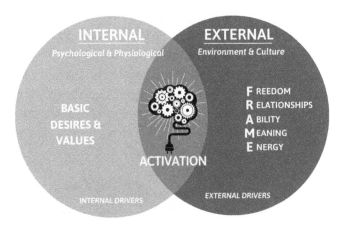

When a person has a clear understanding of their intrinsic values, and has aligned them with their work and activities, they bring confidence and purpose to their interactions with others and to their work environment. The positive energy and collaborative spirit strengthen the external domain, benefiting everyone. When an environment is clear on its purpose, positive, and supportive it reinforces each person's internal motivation mechanisms. As you put in the work to build this cycle over time, it will become self-sustaining. Ultimately, it will require less of your attention because you empowered others to become Activators who keep the flywheel spinning.

ACTIVATOR SKILLS

Up to this point in the book, you have learned a lot about theories and concepts. I've taken you on a short journey through the relevant behavioral and brain science. And while all of that information is necessary to build understanding and an Activator mindset, you need the skill set to put these ideas into action.

The Activator approach can be applied by focusing on three Activator Skills: Connecting, Coaching, and Culturing. Everything an effective leader does to Activate people fits into these three core skills. If you focus and apply these every day, you will create a highly motivated, engaged, and high-performing culture. Each of these skills will strengthen the internal and external mechanisms of your people and build a cycle that optimizes the brains of your people.

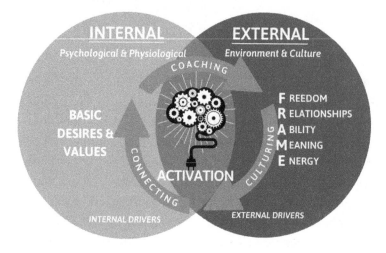

CONNECTING

This is the process of building and cultivating a relationship with each employee that engenders trust and partnership. Connecting creates a pathway of openness, credibility, and vulnerability that opens people up to your leadership. The level of connection we build with employees will ultimately determine the degree to which we can lead and influence the person. In a work environment, Connection is often viewed as a "nice to have" element and is overshadowed by the compulsion to focus on more directive behaviors such as delegation, coaching, and accountability. However, the importance of Connecting cannot be overstated. Without it, the other skills will be hampered.

COACHING

As your connection strengthens, you will become a more effective coach. Coaching is an approach to leadership that uses a collaborative style to lead employees toward achieving their goals. Coaching gives you a method to partner with an employee to develop a plan of action. Applying coaching skills allows you to create and maintain a FRAME environment that activates people to be self-directed, motivated, and deeply engaged in their work.

CULTURING

Culturing is the process of setting, modeling, and upholding the standards of behavior and performance you desire within your team and organization. It is a word you don't hear often, and conveys the idea that you and your employees are actively shaping your culture daily. Activators understand that they don't dictate culture. Rather, they lead the shaping of it through an everyday process. Nothing is more important to the culture than the standards that are set and agreed upon by employees and then sustained through accountability efforts.

These skills do not stand on their own. As you build competency and consistency in one, it builds strength in the others. In the following chapters, I will show you exactly how to be an Activator by implementing tactics for Connecting, Coaching, and Culturing to light-up the brains and unleash the potential of your people.

PART III

ACTIVATION SKILLS

CHAPTER 6
CONNECTING
CULTIVATING TRUST THROUGH RELATIONSHIPS

Your effectiveness as a leader and the highest level of influence you will have on another person hinges on one thing—trust. A person's willingness to follow you will correlate with their belief that you want to help and support them. True loyalty to your leadership is not a result of your title, level of authority, or persuasive ability. It is a response to who you are and how you behave.

Effective leadership isn't the result of business transaction where you exchange a paycheck for high performance. Commitment on the part of an employee will only occur when the person feels valued for who they are, not what they do. Unfortunately, a transactional approach to management is still the most common leadership style in organizations today. Even though the data shows how inefficient and expensive it is.

A Harris Poll asked more than a thousand people what manager issues prompted them to quit their jobs and join other companies. The list below details poor management behaviors and the percentage of people who reported experiencing them.[1] These actions destroy trust and an employee's willingness to give extra effort to their work.

Shows disrespect for employees—53%

Breaks promises—46%

Overworks employees—42%

Has unrealistic expectations—40%

Plays favorites—40%

Gossips about other employees—39%

Is overly critical—37%

Micromanages employees—35%

Doesn't listen to employees—34%

A strong connection between an employee and a leader reduces defensiveness and creates openness for coaching and feedback. In addition, a strong connection with a leader encourages employees to extend goodwill to their colleagues and their own direct reports (if they supervise others), creating a robust web of stable connections. As this web of connection strengthens throughout the team and organization, it creates a culture of trust.

What would it be like to work in an environment with this level of connectedness? Amazing, right? This isn't a pipe dream. While we will never achieve perfection in a relationship, a team, or a culture, we can create connections that that help people enjoy their work and thrive on the job.

HEALTHY CONNECTION

Building a trusting relationship begins by making healthy connections with others. Connection can happen in many ways. You may have a looser connection with one person over another because of how often you work with or see them. You may have a stronger connection with someone with whom you have known for a longer time. You could have a connection with a work contact you haven't met in-person; however, this connection would usually be much shallower than with someone you have spent a great deal of time with. Shallow connections are delicate, yet still viable.

Imagine you hear someone give a strong presentation at a conference. Prior to the conference, you had read one of her books, and found the content helpful. As she speaks, you feel even greater rapport because she is sharing ideas that will help you with a current challenge. At that point, you feel a lot of connection and trust with this person.

Now let's say you approach her after the speech. You wait in a small line to speak with her, and then it's finally your turn. You introduce yourself and begin telling her how much her ideas will help you. As you are talking, she receives a text message and reads it on her phone. You can tell she isn't listening to you and has shifted her focus to the text message. Of course, you understand that a busy person can get distracted, so you stop talking to give her time to focus and then come back to the conversation.

After a moment, she realizes she was distracted and tries to reenter the conversation by asking you a question. But as you answer the question, she sees another person she knows in the room and walks toward that person to greet them. She doesn't look like she's coming back, so you abandon the conversation and walk away. You would feel disrespected and disappointed, right? You may reflect on how you temporarily thought she was a great person, yet now, you no longer feel that way. Your feeling of trust with this person has shifted to skepticism.

This is an example of the fragility of shallow connections. The speaker is human, and she clearly had a lot going on that day. She might have a dozen reasons why she was disrespectful during your interaction. But since the connection was shallow, it wasn't strong enough to survive even one negative interaction.

Connections are only as good as their strength, which is developed over time, through many interactions. The most fundamental skill of an effective leader is their ability to connect with their people. Your ability to connect is the precursor to a trusting relationship that can endure the interactional hiccups, miscommunications, and disagreements that naturally occur between humans.

MOVING FROM THREAT TO THRIVE

Connecting builds trust that earns you the right to give constructive feedback that will be embraced by others as a gift. When we don't feel a sense of connection with our leader, it creates a "threat dynamic." This occurs when our brain perceives experiences as more negative or potentially harmful than they really are.

The human brain is naturally attuned to threats in our environment. These threats can be physical or emotional. When someone who has not built trust with you gives you constructive feedback, your brain will perceive it as a threat and enter the state commonly known as "fight-or-flight." This is a physical response our body creates to prepare us for danger. When this happens, more than 30 hormones hit your bloodstream within a matter of seconds. This chemical cocktail, including adrenaline and cortisol, primes your body for extreme physical activity, like if you had to run away from a bear in the woods.

The neuro-activity of your brain shifts from your frontal lobe to the areas of the brain responsible for survival and physical activity that helps you to fight or flee.

Here's the problem: the prefrontal cortex—the front part of your brain just behind your forehead—is a crucial component of the cortex that manages your executive brain function. If you recall from the lesson on the brain in Chapter 4, we depend on the frontal lobe for managing emotions, making sense out of things, and making smart choices. But during a fight-or-flight episode, a lot of those functions get put on the back burner because the threat response forces us into survival mode. This is why people have a hard time thinking and responding when they have been "put on the spot" or caught off-guard with surprising information.

In this situation, your brain will only bypass a threat response if you have a high level of trust with the other person. That is the key to getting an employee to receive and accept constructive feedback in a healthy way.

It makes sense, right? Think back to a time when you learned to do something that was scary to you—ride a bike, swim, jump off a diving board, or drive a car. You felt fear because you didn't trust the environment and your ability to navigate it. Your brain was experiencing a threat response that put you into a state of fear, and you didn't feel safe. But you were probably able to overcome the fear because you trusted the person teaching you. The trust you had in them—your mom holding onto the bicycle seat or the driving instructor with the calm voice—reminded your brain that you were safe. Similarly, your connection with each employee is the pathway for creating trust and moving them forward with confidence.

THE NEUROSCIENCE OF TRUST

A study conducted by Paul Zak, founding director of the Center for Neuroeconomic Studies, demonstrated the importance of how a leader's interactions with a follower affect their brain.[2] Leaders who expressed empathy, openness, and vulnerability caused an immediate chemical reaction on the part of the follower. The follower's brain released the chemical oxytocin in response to the interaction. Oxytocin is known as the "bonding" chemical. It helps people feel closer to others and increases a person's sense of trust in others.

According to Zak, "Employees in high-trust organizations are more productive, have more energy at work, collaborate better with their colleagues, and stay with their employer longer than people working in low-trust companies. They also suffer less chronic stress and are happier with their lives, and these factors fuel stronger performance."

Other studies by Zak sought to understand what interactions created trust, on the part of employees, leading to greater oxytocin levels. These studies pinpoint the following leadership and management behaviors that can lead to greater trust in the work environment.

Recognition: Recognizing someone's efforts and achievements.

Autonomy: Trusting an employee to figure out how to reach work goals.

Transparency: Sharing information as openly as possible with all employees.

Relationships: Managers who continually build relationships with employees and express concern for the employees' well-being can significantly increase feelings of trust.

Vulnerability: Leaders who extend trust, admit their failures, and ask for feedback stimulate an oxytocin release that fosters cooperation.

A few years ago, I realized that if I wanted to get better at golf, I would need to get lessons from a professional coach. So I scheduled my first lesson with a local pro. When I showed up, the coach took me to the driving range and asked me to hit 8–10 balls so he could evaluate my swing. I proceeded to hit five or six balls and then he stopped me. He paused for a moment, and said, "We need to start from the beginning." Suffice it to say I wasn't happy with that response; I felt an awkward combination of anger and embarrassment.

My coach then spent the next 30 minutes teaching me about the four most fundamental and basic parts of the swing—grip, stance, alignment, and posture. Nearing the end of the lesson, he gave me five balls and asked me to drive them down the center of the range with my five-iron. I followed his instruction, and to my surprise, I hit every ball straight down the middle. Even more surprising, I hit the ball an average of 10 to 15 yards farther each time!

We packed up our golf bags and began walking to the clubhouse. As we walked, he said to me, "I know it can be frustrating to take a step back and focus on the basics. You see, everyone wants me to teach them how to hit the ball farther, straighter, and how to spin the ball back to the hole like the pros. But I can't teach that to someone until they have mastered the fundamentals. Without the basics, the fancy stuff doesn't work."

It was then that I understood the power of fundamentals. Ask any sports or performing arts coach what needs to be done when an individual or team's performance is stagnating or declining and they will tell you, "They need to return to the fundamentals." Coaches say this for two reasons. First, when performance declines, it is likely because the foundational skills have become lost or unstable. Second, the only way to return to high performance is to build back up from the fundamentals.

Connection with people is one of the three fundamental skills of effective leadership. Without it, more advanced leadership skills aren't as effective. Have you ever tried to give constructive feedback to someone with whom you don't have a good relationship? I'm betting it didn't work out so well. The stronger your connection is with another person, the more effective you will be at coaching them, delegating tasks to them, giving them constructive feedback, and holding them accountable. Connecting with people builds the trust that earns you the right to do the more difficult tasks of leadership.

THE 3 ELEMENTS OF CONNECTION

You are likely not as good at connecting as you think you are. Several studies reveal the gap we all have between how we perceive our interpersonal ability and what others perceive it to be. We cannot assume that connection is something we have achieved or assume that it will happen automatically. Instead, we must view it as an important component of effective leadership and be intentional about applying the skill daily.

While there are people who seem to have a natural sense of interpersonal savvy, there are just as many for whom these skills don't come naturally. Interpersonal competence is often found in people who have higher levels of extraversion and conscientiousness, and who have been fortunate to grow up around parents and other significant influencers in their lives who have modeled these social skills.

Whether or not interpersonal savvy is a strength of yours, connecting can be learned. You can become a better leader by building connections through three intentional practices.

Care: Respect, approachability, and support.

Character: Integrity, humility, and mutual benefit.

Communication: Consistency, clarity, and customization.

CARE

Theodore Roosevelt articulated a core principle of human interaction when he said, "People don't care how much you know until they know how much you care." We don't connect with others because of how intelligent, experienced, or talented we are. Nor do we connect because of a title or authority role given to us. People want to grow strong connections with people who show them respect, concern, and support. In fact, encountering the people who display the opposite of these traits repulses us and we want to avoid them. Care is our outward expression that we want the best for others. Care can be demonstrated through our words, but eventually we must go beyond statements of support and show it our actions.

One of the most overlooked components of care is a person's approachability. A recent survey by Ultimate Software found that 50% of employees reported that their manager was approachable. Yet 75% of the 2000 employees surveyed said that approachability was the most important quality in an effective leader.[3]

Let me give you a great example of caring. A few years ago, I worked closely with the president of an organization who truly cared for his people. I was facilitating a training program for his company. During a break, one of the managers wanted to tell me about the president, and what he'd done the prior weekend.

He had learned that a front-line employee was sick and in the hospital. The next day the president took time out of his schedule to visit her. While at the hospital, the president showed great humility and spoke highly of the employee to her family. Before he left, he asked if he could say a prayer for her. Sitting on the woman's bedside with her family, he led a short, heartfelt prayer. The woman who told me the story had tears in her eyes. Then she offered, "That's one of the reasons we work so hard for this company."

Caring comes in many forms. The key is that we have to look for ways to show care to those we want to build connections with. When people believe we want the best for them and seek an outcome that will help them, trust is elevated. Here are a few questions you can ask yourself to determine the level of care you are giving.

⚡ *Do I treat every person with respect?*

⚡ *Do I look for opportunities to show care to my employees?*

⚡ *When I see an employee struggling, do I take time to encourage and support them?*

⚡ *Do I come across as a leader who wants to be served or as a leader who is looking to serve others?*

⚡ *When I have difficult interactions with employees, do I follow up to communicate my care for them and my desire to move forward with a clean slate?*

⚡ *Have I demonstrated a lack of caring? If so, how can I avoid these behaviors in the future?*

CHARACTER

Character is a person's values put into action. Your character is revealed through your daily behavior, not what you say. This perspective provides a way to think about character from a growth perspective, rather than from a belief that it is a fixed trait—you either have it or don't.

Think of a person's character as a set of qualities that demonstrates what they value. We are all familiar with character traits like honesty, integrity, determination, and humility. But there are many more qualities that define who we are as a person and will determine how much people trust us.

Take, for example, an employee who often delivers expense reports riddled with multiple errors. You determine that these errors were simple, and could have been corrected, prior to submission, if the person had taken the time to review the report. While you probably wouldn't say this person has low character or is unethical, you can safely say that they are not thorough. Recognizing that improvement is needed, you can coach the employee on increasing the value they assign to thoroughness and on demonstrating conscientious character by producing work that has been reviewed for errors. In this case, you don't need to train the employee on how to use a calculator or how to review a report. This is why character is an issue of mindset and values, rather than one of skill.

This perspective on character allows you to help people develop and continually build trust with others. As a leader, your character demonstrates your values to people. There are dozens of positive character qualities and not everyone values each one equally. Here are a few that are most often recognized as being important.

- ⚡ Patience
- ⚡ Consistency
- ⚡ Congruence
- ⚡ Timeliness
- ⚡ Kindness

- ⚡ Bravery
- ⚡ Grit
- ⚡ Discipline
- ⚡ Responsibility
- ⚡ Altruism

If people detect that you don't value something they value, they are less likely to trust you. This is especially true for fundamental character qualities like honesty, dependability, and respect. For example, if you have a supervisor who talks poorly about other employees and colleagues, aren't you going to be careful about what you say and do around that person? Your trust in that person will likely be obstructed by their behavior.

Your actions demonstrate your character every minute of every day to the people around you. If an employee perceives poor or inconsistent character in you, their motivation quality and level of engagement will likely decline. In some cases, they may even work against you. Of course, they may also do what you tell them to because you are the boss, but they will likely not do it to the best of their ability. Most humans do not like to support people who behave with poor character.

In contrast, what if you had a supervisor who consistently demonstrated a high level of character? If you have a leader whose actions show respect to everyone and convey honesty, transparency, care, and concern for you, would you regard them with trust? Likely so. What if you had a disagreement with that person about an issue during a meeting? How would you perceive this person? Do you see them as selfish, egotistical, and out for themselves? Likely not. The character of this leader enables you to focus on the topic of disagreement, see different perspectives, and have a healthy discussion rather than wondering about any hidden intention. This is the power of character to build a deep level of trust that fosters positive connections with others.

A few years ago, I conducted a research study investigating the influence of character on employees. I wanted to know if an employee's perception of their manager's character had an impact on their motivation, effort, and engagement at work. I also wanted to know if an employee's perception of the senior management team (the highest level of leaders in the organization) would have an impact on their work.

The study used data collected from employees from more than 30 companies across many industries. Each employee was asked to rate the character of their manager and members of their senior leadership team on statements like, "My supervisor always tells the truth," "My supervisor keeps promises and commitments," "My supervisor acts consistently with the values of our organization," "My supervisor stands up for what is right," and "My supervisor treats everyone with respect."

The data showed that, employees who rated their supervisor's character as high, demonstrated greater effort at work and higher levels of engagement, than their counterparts, who gave their supervisor a lower character rating. The strongest positive correlation was found between the rating of a supervisor's character and an employee's enjoyment of their work.[4]

When looking at the ratings for senior leaders, the data revealed an interesting phenomenon. Although a person's perception of the character of each of the senior leadership team correlated positively with effort and engagement, it was much less significant. This is a great reminder that a person's direct supervisor is likely the most significant influence on the employee's satisfaction, effort, and engagement.

A deeper look into the data found something else. There was a significant positive correlation in the character ratings between supervisors and senior leaders. This was expected. But we were curious to know what the impact would be when a person perceived their senior leadership to be low in character, but their supervisor to be high in character. In almost every case, when a supervisor was rated highly, it didn't matter if the senior leadership team was rated low. Employees' effort, engagement, and enjoyment of work remained high. I began to refer to this phenomenon as "the insulator effect." A direct supervisor's demonstration of character is so powerful that it not only serves as a catalyst for greater effort and engagement, but it also defuses the impact of poor character among senior leadership. This further proves the importance of building a strong connection between yourself and your direct reports. It can significantly impact the motivation, engagement, and performance of your people.

COMMUNICATION

Communication is at the heart of the connection between two people. What should be pointed out, though, is that there is no exact formula for how to communicate effectively to build a strong connection. Communication has so many aspects that it can be overwhelming: It can be verbal or non-verbal, written or oral, formal or informal, one-to-one, or in groups of all sizes. And think of the differences in tone and presentation across memos, letters, emails, text messages, social media posts, small-group meetings, large presentations, or conversations with friends.

I'm not going to give you an in-depth review of every communication skill, and how to build it. There are plenty of great books available that can help you learn to be a better communicator. However, there are a few basic qualities of communication that Activators focus on to enhance their ability to connect.

Eye Contact: You build a deeper connection and increase trust when you make direct eye contact with others. Avoid glancing at your computer, phone, or any other visual distractions.

Body Language: Your body needs to show attentiveness during communication. For instance, sometimes your face and eyes are attentive, yet your body is angled in another direction. When this happens, it communicates that you are in a hurry or not fully engaged.

Expressions: Use facial expressions, sounds, and words to express your concern, care, and attentiveness. Nodding your head, raising your eyebrows, smiling, and frowning all enhance the connection during a conversation. Using words and verbal cues like "hmmm," "ah," "uh-huh," "yes," and "wow" help express your interest.

Listening: Your ticket to effective two-way communication is listening. When you listen, you increase trust and openness with others. And there's no excuse for being a bad listener—it's a skill that can be learned through practice and intention, but only when you commit, and make it a priority. This skill is so important to Activators that we will dive deeper into it in the next chapter.

Inquiry: Asking questions is a great way to both gain information from the other person and help them process and organize their thoughts. Using questions, rather than instruction, is a leadership tool that can create a sense of confidence and ownership on the part of others.

Reflection: Restating what the person says is a method for locking into your memory the details of the conversation. Most importantly, it helps the other person know you are hearing what they say, while also allowing them to hear themselves. To reflect, restate what the person said to you, and make sure you say it in your own words so you don't sound like a robot.

Consistency: You will learn more about communicating strategically when we discuss coaching in the next chapter. But for now, I want you to consider one more thing; the importance of a communication cadence in your leadership. A cadence is a standard or consistent sequence that, when applied over a long period, often becomes a habit. A cadence helps people know what to expect and when to expect communication. Here are a few questions you can ask yourself to evaluate your communication cadence and habits.

⚡ *How often do I communicate one-on-one with each of my employees?*

⚡ *How do I communicate to each of my employees (in person, email, text message, video conference, information drop-in or desk visits, etc.)?*

⚡ *Do I have times where employees know they will have access to me?*

⚡ *Are there any employees who receive more communication from me than others?*

✦ *Are there any employees with whom I don't communicate often? Why?*

Earlier in my career, I was a director at a company that was being acquired by AT&T. After the announcement had been made that we were being purchased, my supervisor, who was the vice president of HR, called me to her office. She told me what I could expect moving forward, and I was pleasantly surprised with the "stay bonus" I would receive if I helped the company transition. Little did I know what that bonus had obligated me to do. She then said, "Jason, your responsibility has been to develop the talent of this company. It has changed. Now your responsibility is to help keep the wheels on this company until the acquisition closes." I didn't realize at that time that acquisitions like this take six to nine months to complete.

During that time, people began leaving the company in droves. As you can imagine, many of them decided to find a job with security rather than waiting to see if they would be offered a job after the acquisition finalized. We wanted to keep employees on the job and performing well, so my team and I began implementing strategies to help people feel better about their situation.

My role also had responsibility for corporate communications, and every week we received dozens of calls and emails from people around the country wanting to know why they hadn't received an update on the acquisition. We continued to tell people we would let them know any information as soon as we received it. But this didn't seem to help, and the distrust was quite evident. Many employees even accused us of withholding information.

One day when we were conducting a focus group luncheon, we were talking to a group of employees about the issue of communication. I was lamenting the fact that we didn't get a lot of information from the acquisition leaders at AT&T due to legal reasons. I said, "It's hard to communicate when you don't have anything to communicate." Then an insightful woman at the table responded, "I think people need consistent and ongoing communication. We would like to know there is nothing new to report." She was absolutely correct. Communication is usually more about the intent than the content.

ACTIVATION WORDS

Numerous research studies have investigated the impact that words have on people's behavior. These studies validate what most of us would guess. The more positive words you use, the more positively people will think and behave. Likewise, the more negative an influencer's words, the more negative their followers' thinking will be.

Psychologist John Bargh focused on using words as primers in his research that investigated the impact of words on people's behaviors. [5] Participants in the study were given a word scramble task, using either words associated with politeness such as respect, courteous, and graciously; or words associated with rudeness such as interrupt, disturb, and obnoxious. The puzzles were used to prime participants to behave in a polite way or a rude way.

Each participant was then asked to take part in a conversation with another person; they were timed to see how long it took the participant to interrupt the other person. The researchers found that the participants who had been primed with rude words interrupted significantly quicker than the participants who had been primed with polite words. More than 60% of the participants primed to be rude interrupted, while less than 20% of the participants primed with polite words did.

A similar study focused on collaboration and showed that people who were primed with words such as cooperation, teamwork, collective, united, share, and trust were willing to be more generous to others and give more to charity.[6]

The power of words isn't limited to what others say to you, or what you say to others. The words we use when talking to ourselves are just as powerful, if not more so. Harvard University professor Alison Wood Brooks has conducted multiple studies on how the use of different words can dramatically affect a person's emotions and performance. In one study, she asked participants who were feeling anxiety about singing karaoke to replace their self-talk of "I am anxious" with "I am excited." A change of one word resulted in people singing 28% better (i.e., with more accuracy) than the control group that continued to tell themselves they were anxious.[7]

In another study Brooks conducted, two groups of participants were asked to complete eight complex math problems under time pressure. One group was instructed to "try to remain calm," while the other was instructed to "get excited." The "get excited" group scored 8% higher on the test than the "remain calm" group. Similar studies have yielded the same results for other performance-based activities.

Words are powerful! While some words can damage, the right words can elevate a person, a team, and a culture. Words that are supportive and positive activates optimal brain function and the release of neurochemicals like dopamine that make us smarter, happier, and more confident. Words that create stress release cortisol, resulting in a state of threat and brain deactivation that leads to lower levels of confidence and performance. I challenge you to think about the words you use often. Are they positive? Do they prime people for the behaviors you want them to demonstrate at work?

Start implementing words in your communication that empower people and foster connection and cooperation. Here are some examples of words you can start integrating into your daily communication that can help activate the positive energy and motivation of the people you lead.

ACTIVATION WORDS

Cooperate	Awaken	Gracious	Accomplish
Collaborate	Invigorate	Courteous	Meaning
Teamwork	Launch	Disciplined	Fulfillment
Trust	Unleash	Courageous	Overcome
Idea	Ambition	Awesome	Prevail
Spark	Stamina	Triumphant	Enterprising
Insight	Vitality	Flexible	Attractive
Passion	Win	Adaptable	Vital
Achieve	Discover	Determined	Dynamic
Share	Compassion	Grow	Fearless
Fun	Alert	Develop	Passionate
Enjoyment	Endurance	Freedom	Conquer
Power	Love	Zest	Flourish
Spirit	Victory	Enthusiastic	Prosper
Revive	Hero	Grateful	Benefit
Refresh	Legacy	Smart	Tough
Create	Respect	Positivity	Accomplish
Rally	Diligence	Impact	Success

CONSTRUCTIVE COMMUNICATION

Do you know someone who rubs you the wrong way, but you can't figure out why? It is likely due to the phrases and words they use. Shelly Gable, a professor at UC Santa Barbara, and her research colleagues have studied speech interactions between people for many years. Their research has led them to discover four distinct ways that people respond to others.[8] Each of the four ways is either active or passive and then either constructive or destructive.

Let's look at examples of each as a response to an employee saying to her supervisor, "I'm so excited, I hit my sales goal early this month!"

	Active	Passive
Constructive	Involved and positive/supportive response to another person's communication. *"That's awesome! I've been seeing your hard work and knew it would pay off for you."*	Uninvolved and positive/supportive response to another person's communication. *"Awesome!"*
Deconstructive	Involved and negative/unsupportive response to another person's communication *"Good, but don't let that make you complacent. We all have to keep working as hard as we can."*	Uninvolved and negative/unsupportive response to another person's communication *"Remember the sales team meeting is starting at 9 a.m. sharp tomorrow."*

Activators use Active Constructive Responses (ACRs) as their default because—consciously or not—they know it activates the brain and creates positive energy. Destructive responses, whether active or passive, are dissonant leadership behaviors that will likely shut down many areas of the brain.

While this is easy to understand, it is more difficult to put into action in a real-life situation. Many leaders use destructive responses because they are managing their own internal battles around ego, insecurity, competitiveness, jealousy, aggression, disappointment, and distraction, among others. Nobody is perfect, but we must monitor our communication to ensure it isn't reflecting our internal battles and harming our employees. To be intentional with our responses, we must set personal principles and standards for how we will respond to others. For example, we might create a personal rule that we won't respond to a negative email within 24 hours. We might also make it a goal to always smile and congratulate someone when they talk about their achievements.

ACTIVATION PHRASES

We can weave words together in such a way that the meaning is profound. While many great writers and orators have used words to touch people's lives, most of us hope to construct phrases that are somewhat grammatically correct and are understood by the person with whom we are communicating. Being an Activator doesn't require extraordinary ability or skill in communication. Words become powerful when you use phrases that communicate a desire and willingness to help and support the success of others, even if you're not the most eloquent person.

Here's an example of two questions that are simple yet powerful.

What do you think?

How can I help you?

These questions communicate respect, dignity, value, and a desire to give support. Questions and phrases like that, Activate the human brain by increasing the perception of safety and unleash the neurochemicals that support optimal cognitive function.

CONNECTING MOTIVATION

Most leaders struggle to understand what motivates their employees. Books and training programs fail to provide practical guidance and tactics about how to understand and utilize intrinsic motivators. Leaders must think beyond extrinsic rewards and recognition and try to understand the deeper intrinsic values of each employee that give them energy and invites deeper engagement in their work.

Early in my career, I thought most employees shared motivations similar to mine. During my early years as a manager, I had an employee that was a single mother. She was an exemplary employee for a long period of time. But then her performance dropped off. I gave her informal feedback a couple of times before having a formal coaching conversation with her. I knew that she had a young daughter who was experiencing some health issues, so I planned to be as understanding and caring as possible, while also holding her accountable for her work.

When we sat down to talk, I began by explaining the performance problems that needed to be addressed. But then instead of coaching it through with her and getting her perspective, I began to project my motivations onto her. With infinite wisdom, I made statements like, "I can really see you moving into a management role one day if we can get your performance back on track" and, "you have great potential for moving up to more responsibility."

I thought my words would energize and encourage her, but I was wrong. Her eyes began to water and she said, "Jason, I couldn't care less about a management role right now; I'm just trying to make it through each day caring for my daughter and getting her well." I was speechless. I was wrong to believe she valued what I valued. Chalk that one up to a big mid-twenties' learning moment.

THE SIXTEEN BASIC DESIRES

I introduced you to the 16 Basic Desires in chapter 3, but now I want to show you how you can use the sixteen desires to better understand and connect with your people. This approach gives us a simple and scientific way to understand what truly motivates your employees. Not only does it help us understand them, but it gives us a way to connect a person's work with what they find to be meaningful and purpose-driven. As a reminder, here is the list of the 16 basic desires and their definitions.

Acceptance: The desire for positive self-regard.

Beauty: The desire for aesthetically appealing experiences.

Curiosity: The desire for understanding.

Eating: The desire to consume food.

Family: The desire to raise children and spend time with siblings.

Honor: The desire for upright character.

Idealism: The desire for social justice.

Independence: The desire for self-reliance.

Order: The desire for structure and stability.

Physical Activity: The desire for muscle exercise.

Power: The desire for influence of will.

Saving: The desire to collect things.

Social Contact: The desire for companionship with peers.

Status: The desire for respect based on social standing.

Tranquility: The desire to avoid experiencing anxiety and pain.

Vengeance: The desire to confront those who frustrate or offend us.

Using the 16 desires to understand your people has some nuances, but give me a few minutes, and I will open your eyes to how easy it is to apply it to your leadership.

Each desire is measured by your level of intensity on a continuum from weak to strong. Many of your desires will fall into the average range. An average desire means that it is important from time to time, but it isn't a significant focus in your life. Desires that have a strong or weak intensity will be a significant motivator and will occupy your thoughts and guide your behaviors. You will focus (and sometimes obsess) about fulfilling your strong and weak desires. It is easy for people to see your weak and strong desires as they can be seen consistently in your behavior; they are a highlight of your personality and define your sense of fulfillment.

We can think about each desire on a continuum. Using the image below, you can see that Sue has a weak desire for Power, Tom has an average desire, and Pam has a strong desire for it. Each person's level of intensity can help us predict who will be delighted to take on a leadership role and who will avoid it. Because a desire is a motivation to value a particular belief or behavior, we can predict that Sue's weak desire for power means she will not be motivated to take on a leadership role and act as an influencer. She will not find enjoyment or fulfillment in power-oriented positions. Conversely, Pam's strong desire for power leads us to believe that she will not only enjoy being influential, she will also pursue these behaviors naturally in her behavior. Leadership is meaningful and intrinsically rewarding to her.

POWER

The desire for Influence or leadership

WEAK DESIRE	AVERAGE DESIRE	STRONG DESIRE
Sue	Tom	Pam

Now look at Tom. His level of intensity for Power is in the average range. He will sometimes enjoy being influential depending on the situation. He can do it and can be successful in exhibiting power behaviors. However, his motivation for leading and influence won't always be high, and he won't always find great meaning and fulfillment in taking on these types of roles.

Each of the basic desires can be measured to determine the level of a person's desire intensity. IDS Publishing Corporation has the only thoroughly reliable and validated comprehensive assessment to measure each of the desires. The assessment is called the *Reiss Motivation Profile*® (ReissMotivation-Profile.com), commonly referred to as the RMP. It is an online motivation assessment that provides you with extensive feedback on your desires, values, and motives. This is particularly helpful for executive and leadership coaching and development feedback sessions. A team report is also available providing you with a map of a team's motivations, compatibilities, gaps, and potential conflicts. You can learn more about taking the assessment for yourself or your team at *DrJasonJones.com/RMP*

If you aren't quite ready to take the RMP assessment but want to have a general idea of your motives and value, you can take the *Motives & Values Quiz* at *TheActivatorBook.com/MVQ*. This is a quick way to help you think through each desire and get a preliminary list of your top motivators.

It would benefit you to take your understanding of Basic Desires deeper by reading, *The Normal Personality: A New Way of Thinking About People*[9] and *Who Am I? The 16 Basic Desires That Motivate Our Actions and Define Our Personalities.*[10] Both authored by Steven Reiss, Ph.D.

MOTIVATION PROFILING

Now that you know how to assess each of your own desires, you can apply the assessment to understand the motivations of others. The process by which you study and seek to understand the intrinsic motivators of others is called **motivation profiling**. This process gives us a better way to understand where people generate internal energy.

Let's use Steve Jobs as an example of how we profile someone's motivations. I rated each of the desires for him. Please note that I didn't know Jobs when he was alive nor have I ever met him. I'm basing my assessment solely on his biography written by Walter Isaacson. I used a worksheet called the Motives and Values Profile to rate him for each of the desire.

MOTIVATORS	WEAK	AVG	STRONG
Acceptance – the desire for positive self-regard	✓		
Beauty – the desire for aesthetically appealing experiences			✓
Curiosity – the desire for understanding		—	
Eating – the desire to consume food		—	
Family – the desire to raise children and spend time with siblings		—	
Honor – the desire for upright character	✓		
Idealism – the desire for social justice		—	
Independence – the desire for self-reliance		—	
Order– the desire for structure and stability		—	
Physical Activity – the desire for muscle exercise		—	
Power – the desire for influence of will			✓
Saving – the desire to collect things		—	
Social Contact – the desire for companionship with peers		—	
Status – the desire for respect based on social standing			✓
Tranquility – the desire to avoid experiencing anxiety and pain	✓		
Vengeance – the desire to confront those who frustrate or offend			✓

Below I have listed the Basic Desires that seemed to be his key motivators. These are the areas which he is intrinsically valued. When Jobs was pursuing these desires, he was motivated and more likely to be engaged. His focus and pursuit of the desires below formed his personality and sense of purpose. They defined what made life worth living and what activities held meaning in his life.

Acceptance – WEAK: He was very self-confident and didn't allow setbacks to deter him from striving for success and reaching his goals.

Beauty – STRONG: He wanted Apple to create beautiful computers, not brown boxes.

Honor – WEAK: He didn't hold himself to traditional business rules and norms. He seemed to find satisfaction in behaving in rebellious ways.

Power – STRONG: He had an internal drive to influence and lead others.

Status – STRONG: He was highly concerned with his reputation and the prestige that comes with founding and leading technology companies.

Tranquility – WEAK: He thrived during times of stress and was easily bored.

Vengeance – STRONG: He enjoyed competing and didn't shy away from conflict.

Now you can use a similar process to think about each of your employees, peers, family members, or anyone else you'd like to understand better. You can download a copy of the Motives and Values Profile (MVP) worksheet at *TheActivatorBook.com/Resources*. I encourage you to have conversations with your employees that are exploratory in nature. Ask them questions that help you to get to know their values and motives. Getting to know your employees through conversations and observations will increase the accuracy of your profiling. When you are rating an employee, think about their behavior. What sticks out to you about their values and personality? Don't assume they have a strong or weak desire based one observation. A person's values can only be validated by multiple instances of consistent behavior.

For example, if an employee talks often, or obsessively, about something they learned about or a new book they have read, you can assume that the person is strong in curiosity. Conversely, if an employee grumbles about a training program with mandatory attendance or verbalizes disdain for reading about new ideas, you can assume they are weak in curiosity. If you don't feel you can rate a desire accurately, then mark it as average. This is a safe bet because you usually see a person's strong and weak desires without looking for them.

EMBRACING UNIQUENESS

Your ability to understand the motivations and values of the people you lead is a powerful skill. It will allow you to have deeper insights into what activities and tasks a person will find personally valuable and therefore generate long-term, intrinsic energy. When a person is involved in tasks that are meaningful to them, they are more likely to engage in their work. Another reason that understanding the motivations of others is so powerful is because it helps you to identify the uniqueness of a person and the differences between people. This allows you to delegate and coach each person more effectively. You can help each of your employees better understand their unique intrinsic motives and help them guide their own behaviors, leading them towards greater happiness and fulfillment.

Steve Jobs is a great example. He had a unique combination of a weak desire for acceptance coupled with a strong desire for power and beauty. This profile explains many of the motives and behaviors that were the essence of who Steve Job was as a human and a business leader. His lack of concern for what others thought of him allowed him to think differently and to be confident in his unique ideas. Now, add the fact that he had a strong desire for Beauty and you can see why he was so passionate about changing computers from brown boxes to beautifully crafted technology. He found such great intrinsic value in beauty that he wanted Apple product packaging and the customer unboxing process to be a beautiful and memorable experience.

Motivation profiling can be a powerful tool to understand your motivations, core values, and behaviors. It can also be a powerful tool to help you understand the people you live with, work with, and lead. Everyone is trying to assert the values they hold most dear to them through their behavior.

CONNECT TO ACTIVATE

Becoming an Activator starts by connecting with your employees. When people believe that you care about them and feel a personal connection with you, their trust soars. While our reptilian brain judges people on the basis of similarity and familiarity, our cerebral cortex empowers us to make deeper connections that create lasting relationships. This only happens when we use our brain to understand and embrace the differences between people. In doing this, we are able to leverage the diversity of the motives and values of people around us.

We become better as individuals and team members as we move beyond our brain's survival mode and practice care, character, and communication to build strong bonds with others. It cultivates openness and paves the way for interactions, experiences, and coaching that unleash people from their fear and defensiveness. By leveraging the differences of our people, we free them to do their best and we harness the strengths of our team and organization.

BRAIN ACTIVATION - CONNECTING TACTICS

 Create Safety with Simple Behaviors. Smile more. Make direct eye contact. Relax. Use touch appropriately.

 Use Power Words. Be intentional with the words you use. Before meetings (one-on-one or group) write down 3-5 positive words you want to use within the first five minutes of the meeting.

 Use Power Phrases. Use phrases that inject positivity and encouragement to others. Phrases can take the form of questions that facilitate interaction and build trust. Take time to write one or two power phrases that you want to use consistently and begin working them into your communication with others.

 Extend Trust. Relinquish control over certain responsibility areas. Empower people by extending trust by assigning specific responsibilities. Use power phrases like, "I have full confidence in you."

 Show Vulnerability. Don't try to be perfect. Let your employees know what skills you are working to develop and how you are getting better. Never blame others. Show emotion. Express feelings. Use power phrases like, "I don't know, let's figure this out together," and "I need your help."

 Demonstrate Transparency. Communicate with authenticity. Look people in the eyes. Avoid distraction. Ask people if they have questions and ask about their concerns. Communicate consistently and often. Avoid starting a sentence with, "Honestly…" or "To tell you the truth." Use power phrases like, "What else would you like to know?" and "I'll always be open and honest with you." Then back these statements up with action.

Be Available. Allow your calendar to be seen by employees and colleagues. Set consistent blocks of time on your calendar for support and impromptu meetings. Use power phrases like, "What else would you like to know?" and "How can I help you?"

Banish Bias. Be an advocate for diversity and inclusivity. Call out biases, prejudices, and assumptive thinking when you see it in yourself and others. Challenge employees to think differently and avoid fear-based decisions and actions. Praise those who question the status quo. Use power phrases like, "What are you (we) not thinking about?", "Let's look at this from a different perspective," and "How can you (or we) leverage all our knowledge, experiences, and skills?"

Encourage Self-Expression. Remind people that you want to hear their unique perspectives and insights. Invite them to question the status quo. Encourage each person to bring their authentic selves to work each day and contribute with confidence.

Show Empathy. Express your concern. Feel the emotions they are feeling. Use verbal sounds to express understanding. Use body language and facial expressions to demonstrate emotion (surprise, excitement, happiness, disappointment, rejection, anger, etc.). Instead of asking employees, "How are you doing?" ask, "What are you experiencing?"

Explore Values and Desires. Facilitate a discussion that helps your employee to identify their values. Ask them about their current priorities. Make connections between their values, desires, and their work.

Allow Job Crafting. Allow employees to create or update their own job descriptions. Help them shape their role, responsibilities, and goals to harness their skills, strengths, character, interests, and passions.

Opportunities Assessment. Similar to a threat assessment, but focused on questions regarding opportunities and ideas. Ask employees about what opportunities exist that can help them progress and succeed at work. Ask them what they like about their work.

Connect and Introduce. Introduce employees to people you know inside and outside of your organization. Help them grow their professional network. Invite an employee to a networking event.

Check-in Meetings. Hold consistent one-on-one meetings with your employees on a regular basis (e.g., once a week or once every two weeks). Use the time to check-in on work projects, goal progress, and monitor development. Be careful not to cancel these meetings too often due to something more important.

Get to Know You (GTKY) Meetings. Meet with employees and let them know the agenda is just about getting to know them better. Use appropriate questions like, "What is most important to you? What activities do you enjoy outside of work? What are you passionate about?" Be careful not to ask intrusive personal questions. Use generic questions that are open-ended and prompt employees to share at their current level of trust.

 Identify and Praise Progress. Create and maintain momentum and motivation by pointing out the progress a person is making on a project, goal, a change, or skill development. Even small wins and progress light up the brain and create energy and confidence.

 Communicate with Active-Constructive Responses. Assess the way you respond to people in times of stress and when people share their ideas and achievements. Take time to think through how you want to respond in an Active-Constructive way in all situations.

 Gift a Resource. Periodically give an employee (individual or as a group) a resource that can help them pursue their goals and create success and growth. You could give a book, a training program on an area of interest, bring in a guest speaker, set up a one-on-one coaching session for an employee with another leader, or send someone to a conference or professional meeting.

CHAPTER 7
COACHING

FACILITATING HIGH-PERFORMANCE WITH BACKBONE AND HEART

Coaching is a skill that activates a higher level of thinking and action on the part of employees. We will dive into these skills in a few minutes. Before doing so, let's take a moment to level-set.

Being an effective coach starts with your heart. I'm always amazed at how good people are at detecting a person's true intent. Human intuition has evolved over millennia to be good at detecting whether a person has good or ill intent. This is especially true at work.

Coaching is an approach to leading performance that draws upon positive intent for helping a person grow and develop. If you are disinterested in helping someone, they will see it. But if you truly want to help your employees do their best, the coaching approach can help you execute the most challenging and uncomfortable tasks of leadership.

I have spoken to many people who tell me their bosses seem nice and friendly when things are going well. But when things aren't going well, they become demanding and threatening. People use words like intense, mean, obsessive, passive-aggressive, and even aloof to characterize their leaders in the midst of a crisis.

Stress is the true test for the heart and authenticity of a leader. How you interact with your employees during stressful times communicates more about your character and your values than any words stated or written. When people see you abandon respectfulness and become an adversary through behaviors that lack emotional intelligence and discipline, they perceive you as being inauthentic and self-centered. They know your focus is really your achievement, not theirs.

You can eloquently communicate your leadership values and purpose by telling your people how much you care and want to support their success. But none of those words matter if they see contrary behavior from you. Trust is easy to destroy when you say one thing and do another. Activators understand that every interaction is important.

WHAT KIND OF COACH ARE YOU?

I decided to play football when I was in 4th grade. I showed up, all four-foot five inches and 65 pounds of me, at Highland Park elementary school, ready to be the next football all-star. As I went through the process of checking out my pads, I realized that I was the smallest kid on the team. I decided to move forward and take my chances.

After the first week of practice, I was ready to quit. I felt I couldn't play very well; I felt inadequate. So I waited until after the practice was over and everyone had left the field except for Coach King. I told him that I was going to quit and that I would return my pads once we got back into the locker room.

I fully expected my announcement to be a relief to him. To my surprise, Coach King asked, "Why? You are doing great, and I like you being out here." I remember explaining to him,

"I just don't think I'm good enough. I don't even have a position." I'll never forget him saying with emphasis, "We will find you a spot!" I felt a little better and decided to stay on the team.

Over the next week, Coach King tried me at different positions and he finally determined that the best place for me was at the running back position. The first game arrived, and we were all excited. When the game began, I learned that I was a starter! Well, I was a starter on the second string of the "B-Team." "A-Team" was composed of the bigger kids, while B-Team was the smaller kids. The first-stringers were the group of kids that played first, while second-stringers played later. The schedule was set up to allow all the kids to get time on the field.

There were four minutes left in the second quarter and I was finally getting my turn. I was nervous. As I walked to my first real game football huddle, Coach King called the play. It was a 38 Sweep. The play ran through my head and then it registered in my brain, *I am the "3" back and that means the quarterback is going to toss me the ball and I am supposed to run around the right end (the 8 hole). Yikes!*

Fear overwhelmed me. I wasn't sure if I was going to be able to catch the quarterback's toss, much less remember what to do after that. I thought about the 11 guys on the other side of the ball who might want to take my life by slamming me into the ground and piling on top of me.

We lined up, and the ball was hiked to the quarterback. I ran to the right while looking at the quarterback. He tossed the ball to me. It was only about 3 feet, but back then, it felt like ten. I caught it, tucked it under my right arm, and began to run around the right end of the line.

It was then that I noticed three large, heavily padded angry opponents, running at me. I'm pretty sure smoke was coming from their ears and fire was shooting from their nostrils. As I ran toward the sideline in fear, I made an unconscious mental calculation that their angle on me plus their speed was going to beat me to the sideline. This is where I like to say raw talent took over, but in reality, it was an innate survival mechanism.

As they got within a few feet of me, I stuck my right foot into the ground as hard as I could and stopped on a dime. It turns out that stopping quickly is one of the few strengths of a sixty-five pounder. The evil defenders chasing me fell to the ground as they tried to stop. They formed a nice three-man pile right next to the sideline. While they were falling to the ground, I cut back to my left and continued running up the field. There was nothing in front of me, except weeds, dirt, and the end zone. I ran like my life depended on it and scored a touchdown.

I vividly remember running to the sideline and seeing Coach King smiling ear-to-ear. He gave me a wink as if to say, "I told you so." I scored several touchdowns that season. All of them using the same play. Each time I ran to the right, stopped on a dime, and cut up field. You stick with what works, right!

Coach King continued to coach me throughout elementary school. He was one of those coaches who had learned how to strike the delicate balance of driving performance while also caring for his players. Everyone knew that Coach King had our best interest at heart when he push us to do better.

A few years later, I played for my school's freshman team. The head coach was emotionally and physically abusive to us. The year prior, the team composed of the same players and had a winning season. But this year, several players had decided not to return because of the coach. We had extremely low morale that year, and a losing record.

We were playing one of the final games of the year, and I remember wishing the season was over. We had lost too many games. Football no longer felt fun. Mid-way through the second quarter, I was a cornerback on defense. The running back from the opposing team had just cut through the middle of the line untouched. He juked a linebacker, leaving me to be the last line of defense. If I didn't tackle him, he would score.

Somehow, I was able to take him to the ground and saved the touchdown. As I was getting up, I heard a man's voice say, "Great tackle, Jason!" It was the referee. It's extremely rare to hear a referee praise a player. But the voice was familiar. When I looked up, I was surprised to see that it was Coach King! He was moonlighting as a referee.

I sprung up off the ground and said hello, before heading back to my position with a pep in my step. I had more energy and a new vigor I hadn't felt in many games. I went on to play harder than any game that entire season. Why? Because I was playing for Coach King. I wanted him to see who I had become and how I had improved. I wanted him to be proud and to know his investment in me had been worth it.

The difference between Coach King and my freshman coach is stark. It highlights the fact that people want to do and be their best when they are in the presence of people who support them and who have invested in them. Effective leaders are those who have coached and invested in people; in return, they are rewarded with people who play their hearts out.

LEADING WITH BACKBONE AND HEART

When managers and leaders use a coaching approach effectively, they build a powerful relationship dynamic that benefits both parties. Great leaders don't just get results; they impact lives. A coaching approach is the best way to balance driving results with caring for people.

Richard Boyatzis and Anthony Jack, researchers at Case Western Reserve University, studied the impact of coaching on a group of college students.[1] The study paired academic coaches with students. One cohort of students received a coach who purposefully used a "coaching for compliance" approach. The students in the other cohort received a coach who purposefully used a "coaching with compassion" approach. After coaching, students who had received both styles noted that they were helpful. However, a follow-up survey was used to gain deeper insights from the students. It found that students who had a compliance-oriented coach felt the coach induced feelings of guilt and obligation. These coaches were also perceived to be more abrasive. Coaches who had used a compassionate approach were considered more inspirational, trusting, and caring.

Brain scans of the students using functional magnetic resonance imaging (fMRI) found that students with a compassionate coach had more activation in three regions: the lateral visual cortex, which is affiliated with visioning; the ventral striatum and nucleus accumbens, which are affiliated with motivation; and the ventral medial prefrontal cortex, which helps module stress response. Compassionately coached students also were found to have greater left-dominant asymmetry in frontal activation, which is associated with emotions that are more positive. Finally, greater activity was found in the medial parietal cortex where a sense of emotional and social connection occurs. These students exhibited more positive and social-friendly brain responses.

In comparison, compliance coaching resulted in activation of the para-cingulate cortex, which is responsible for managing the threat and stress response. This also activated the medial prefrontal area, which is responsible for feelings of self-consciousness, potentially leading to lower levels of confidence.

Take a moment to think about the best leader you have ever followed. They are probably someone who cared for you but also refused to let you become stagnant. Too many leaders are unbalanced, favoring one side or the other. Some are too heart-heavy. They are great people who are nice, yet they fear confrontation or making someone feel bad. Unfortunately, leaders who are too heart-heavy are reluctant to give constructive feedback or hold people accountable for their results. That part of the job is stress inducing for them because of their approach to leadership.

On the other hand, leaders who are too backbone-heavy care little about people. Their driving behaviors focus on results at all costs, and they come across as uncaring, cold, and distant. Their strength is hitting numbers, while their weakness is keeping people engaged long-term. These leaders often hit their numbers in the near-term, but have problems keeping people engaged in the long-term that results in costing the organization time, resources, and money.

Activators demonstrate a balance of backbone and heart in their interactions. They know that the best way to create long-term results that produce trust and engagement is to use a coaching approach that brings out the best in people. Sets clear expectations, encourage a plan of action, provide support, and empower each employee to reach their goals. Consistency, coupled with a strong connection with each employee, allows you to be honest and direct with people and still maintain a perception of supportiveness and care. The benefits are powerful and include the following outcomes.

- ⚡ Builds trust with direct reports

- ⚡ Demonstrates respect

- ⚡ Guides goal-oriented action

- ⚡ Creates clarity for goals and expectations

- ⚡ Prompts deeper thinking for the problem or challenge

- ⚡ Engenders buy-in to mission, vision, goals, priorities, and action

- ⚡ Builds a sense of ownership and self-direction in people

- ⚡ Reduces a direct report's dependency

- ⚡ Empowers people to take initiative, be creative, and innovate

- ⚡ Develops employee job skills

- ⚡ Teaches and models an effective way to interact with colleagues

- ⚡ Creates a coaching culture where everyone uses similar methods to lead and support others

Coaching is an interactive approach where you play the role of a partner and a guide, depending on the situation. While traditional leadership relied heavily on telling people what to do, coaching utilizes two critical skills: listening and inquiry. Both skills are applied to the interaction to develop and support the growth of the employee.

Coaching conversations focus on allowing the employee to think, process, and make his or her own decisions, rather than being told what to do or how to handle a situation. While there are times, when you need to tell someone what to do or how to do something, coaching creates ownership and self-direction on the part of the employee. It also leads to employee growth and elevated confidence.

The coaching conversation can take place anywhere and is often most effective when it's not located in an office. Coaching is a "real-time" activity. It can be done at any time. I did a lot of my coaching while walking with employees from one place to another. Often between meetings.

The coaching conversation is composed of four key steps. The process begins with ensuring you and your employee are clear on the outcomes you both want. Goal alignment is critical for moving forward together. As they talk, you can use questions to inspire your employee to think deeper and discover the best direction for their work. The next steps get the employee to determine options and obstacles and then create an action plan. Finally, the coaching conversations should include a method of accountability, follow-up, and support that helps the employee know how well they are handling responsibility.

Coaching isn't just encouragement. It's not just setting an expectation and a timetable. True coaching occurs when the leader challenges a person to identify a specific goal and take action to reach it. It is a system of accountability and support, that is created together, to achieve greater commitment, motivation, engagement, and achievement.

THE GOAL MODEL

It is helpful to have a proven coaching model to guide your conversations and interactions with the professionals you lead. The model I use is called "GOAL."

This model is easy to remember, provides a structured process for progression, and gives you a consistent approach you can use over and over again. Let's take a deeper look at how we achieve each step of the GOAL conversation.

Goal – The first step in the coaching process is to ensure each employee has a goal. Many people find it difficult to focus on one specific objective. As a coach, you want to help the employee define the outcome that he or she wants to achieve. The goal can take many forms. It could be hitting a certain sales number, finishing a project by a certain date, or improving a relationship with a colleague. It's important to know that the goal can be created by the person or provided by the leader. If it is set by you, use your coaching skills, which we will talk about in a few minutes, to gain acceptance and buy-in. You want to achieve alignment and agreement on the goal you are working on before you can move forward to the next step of the conversation.

The point of the Goal step is to make sure the focus is set for a productive coaching conversation to occur. You can use the following questions to guide the person you are coaching toward goal clarity.

- *What do you want to focus on?*
- *What is your goal?*
- *What outcome do you want?*

Options – Once the goal is determined, the coach needs to help the employee discover options or available opportunities that will guide him or her toward the goal. It is important that you challenge the employee to think deeply and use his or her imagination to determine all the possible options. Allow the person to come up with ideas before you provide your own ideas. The person will be much more likely to "buy-in" to his or her own options and remain more involved throughout the process.

⚡ *What are the possible ways you can reach your goal?*

⚡ *What creative actions can you take to reach your goal?*

⚡ *Which options/opportunities will enable you to move towards your goal?*

It is important to consider any obstacles that may occur while discussing options for reaching the goal. Ask questions that can help your direct report anticipate barriers that might prevent the option from being viable. For example, an employee may want to build competency in a new coding language by taking an accelerated course in another city. While this is certainly an option, you might want to ask, "What obstacles might get in the way of using this option?" Then let them answer. This is a much better way of conveying your skepticism, which wants to say, "Good luck getting the budget money to do that!" Questions like these can help lead your direct-report to consider potential obstacles.

⚡ *What might get in the way?*

⚡ *What are we not thinking about?*

⚡ *What are the potential obstacles to that option?*

Action Plan – After the options/opportunities have been discussed, it is now time for your employee to create a plan of action for reaching their goal. As a coach, you should challenge the employee to determine and plan his own path forward. This will include writing down action steps, resources, and a timeline. Below are a few questions you may want to use.

⚡ *What are the most viable options/opportunities?*

⚡ *What needs to be the first step?*

⚡ *Which resources will you need?*

Leverage Accountability – Now that your employee has an action plan and a clear next step, it is time to build a system of accountability. Accountability methods stimulate the brain and support motivation toward goal achievement. At a minimum, you want to set a date and time for you to follow up with your employee to review their progress and to encourage them further. You will also need to determine what kind of accountability is necessary to support their achievement— hard or soft accountability.

Hard accountability is typically used when a person's performance and behavior is causing a problem or when the employee hasn't responded with improvement after prior coaching conversations and feedback.

Hard accountability requires,

1) A clear expectation for the goal/result

2) A timeline or deadline for meeting the goal/result

3) A reward for achieving the goal/result

4) Consequences for not achieving the goal/result

Soft accountability is typically used in an initial coaching conversation that addresses a problem with behavior or performance. It is also used for professional development coaching conversations. Soft accountability uses follow-ups, progress check-ins, and verbal cues to refocus the employee on the goal.

You can also employ tactics that are fun. One experience sticks out clearly in my mind, because of how well it worked. I coached a young leader who had risen quickly to a director position in a large organization. He had created a professional goal, to go back to school and earn a college degree. Over a period of months, he had not made any progress on this goal. In fact, he had not even enrolled in any classes. I asked him, "Is this goal still important to you?"

He responded, "Yes, of course!"

Then I asked, "Why haven't you done anything about it?" After he made an excuse about time, I asked, "Would you like for me to implement some accountability for you other than just a progress check-in?" He thought for a moment and then agreed. I then asked him, "What can I do to make sure you take action within the next two weeks?" He couldn't think of anything so I said, "I've got an idea! If you haven't enrolled in your classes by the time we meet in two weeks, I will take the clock on the wall. It will be mine until you do."

He broke a big smile and said, "You really know how to get me moving, don't you? Deal!" You see, the face of this clock was the logo of his favorite college football team. It happened to be a rival of my favorite football team. We'd had many fun rivalry conversations about our teams over the previous few weeks, and I knew how much he would not want me to take his clock. Who knows what I might do to it?

Two weeks later, I walked into the gentleman's office. His first action was to pull a piece of paper out of a folder and proudly hand it to me. It was his enrollment receipt. With a grin, he said, "I don't know if you are brilliant or if it was just happenstance, but every time I looked at my clock to get the time, I remembered that you might try to take it from me!"

There are many ways to apply soft accountability. Be creative with your employee and find something that isn't overly threatening but also creates a small amount of urgency. If you can toss in a small dose of fun, that makes it even better.

Finally, as you complete the Leverage Accountability step, you will want to encourage your employee by stating your confidence in them and offering continual support. This is a great time to remind them of their past successes when they have been committed and focused. Here are some questions you could ask while in this step of the conversation.

⚡ *What will you have accomplished by this time next week?*

⚡ *How will you measure your success?*

⚡ *How can I hold you accountable?*

Using each step of this model will ensure that you continue to progress in the coaching conversation and move the person toward a plan and action. As with any framework or model, allow it to be a guide, not a cage. As you practice and gain experience, it will become more natural for you. Just like riding a bike, the process and the steps will become a natural part of how you lead people. The results of your approach will be on full display as you see your employees demonstrate the following attitudes and behaviors.

- ⚡ Autonomy for action
- ⚡ Responsibility for their decisions and actions
- ⚡ Deeper thinking and processing
- ⚡ Feeling respected and valued
- ⚡ Confidence in their ability
- ⚡ Buy-in for the direction of the team and organization
- ⚡ Generation of new ideas and perspectives
- ⚡ Respect for the way you manage and lead
- ⚡ Leading and activation of others

COACHING SKILLS

Activators continually improve their coaching ability through the development and practice of five coaching skills. The skills include Listening, Inquiry, Giving Feedback, Challenging, and Commending. Each of these skills can be used inside and outside of a coaching conversation. When you use them during the coaching process, they help you progress through the GOAL model steps.

LISTENING

Listening is the foundation of being an effective coach. It is truly the beginning point. I have conducted dozens of coach training workshops and participants have told me that they initially thought they knew all there was to know about listening and that they had discounted the value of it as a skill to develop.

You have likely heard of the two most popular listening modes, passive and active. Passive is the listening you do while your mind is elsewhere. People usually can tell that you are not completely focused or fully engaged in the conversation. Active listening, on the other hand, is done with intent, showing appropriate eye contact and body language to represent your interest and understanding.

There is another type of listening that coaches do. It is a mode of listening that is even deeper. It's called *Deep Listening*. Deep listening occurs when a person actually enters the listening activity with a mindset to hear beyond the words. Deep listening is discovery-oriented as you seek to understand their thinking and identify their beliefs and assumptions that may be hindering their progress. This mode of listening prompts you to focus intently and ask discovery questions. Here are four ways to listen deeply.

Listen for words that give clues. Listen for words that don't fit with the sentence, are possible over-statements, or are highly emotional. These words give clues that the person may be confused, is misunderstanding the situation, or needs to process certain aspects of his or her current beliefs.

Avoid getting lost in your own thoughts. This takes intention and a lot of practice. You must commit to being in a coaching mindset for a certain amount of time. You might say to yourself, *Okay, I'm giving this person 10 minutes of my undivided attention.* You are deciding to move your mind away from your own agenda and thoughts and engage deeply in the words, body language, and emotion being communicated by the person you are coaching.

Avoid making assumptions. Our human nature wants to fill in the gaps of what we don't see or understand. Couple this with the fact that we have our own set of experiences and opinions, and they produce assumptions. Assumptions are ideas we believe to be true without evidence that supports the idea as a fact. As coaches, we have to avoid assuming we know the right answer, or what things a person should do, in a given situation. While we may often know the answer, we must use our other coaching skills to help the person develop and find his or her own way.

Use Silence. Many of us fear the dreaded "dead spots" of conversations. But silence can be a good thing. It can be used as a tool in coaching. Not only does it give a person time to ponder and respond, but it also prompts the person to think deeper. Challenge yourself to use silence during meetings and conversations. Start with smaller amounts of periods of silence and as you become comfortable with it, increase the time you give to it. Done right, this can be a great way to demonstrate your confidence as a coach and leader.

INQUIRY

Activators leverage inquiry as a powerful tool to promote self-direction and ownership of the action plan. When you listen deeply to people, you are naturally led to ask questions that help them clarify their goals and create a step-by-step plan that will lead them to goal achievement. Of the five key coaching skills, questioning may be the most difficult to master. I have not met anyone who is naturally gifted with the ability to ask great questions. What I have found while training many leaders is that the skill of questioning must be developed over a period of time through deliberate practice.

Ask questions that encourage discovery. The role of inquiry is to help a person gain clarity of the situation, think deeper, expand perspectives, and help you, as the coach, better understand his or her situation. The number one rule for inquiry that leads to these outcomes is to ask open-ended questions. In other words, don't ask questions that can be answered with one or two words. Your objective is not only to increase your understanding, but also to help the person discover and commit to their own path of goal achievement.

Be curious about their world. Put yourself into a mindset of listening and learning. Seek to learn about the person and understand exactly what they are experiencing. In this mindset, you will find it easier to ask useful questions. When you catch yourself thinking, *"What is a good question to ask next?"* remind yourself to listen deeply, be curious, discover, and enjoy the process.

Be conversational. It's important to help the person you coach feel relaxed. Use positive body language, smile, and make appropriate eye contact. Allow a two-way dialogue to occur. Think of the process as if you are talking to a friend and helping them with a challenge. After all, that is exactly what you are doing.

Create default questions for each step of the Goal Model. This is a great way to build a repertoire of questions you can easily remember. I have provided a list of coaching questions here for each of the four GOAL steps. Take some time to read each question in each of the section. Then highlight two to three questions in each area that you can see yourself using when you coach. Read through your list of preferred questions before having your next coaching conversation. It will not take long before these questions become natural and easy to use.

Practice, practice, practice. Challenge yourself to practice asking questions as much as possible. You can do this at home, with friends, on the job, or anywhere you are conversing with others. Resolve to use these conversations to practice inquiry. To get a free copy of the questions below, along with other useful coaching questions, download the *Coaching Questions Quick-Reference* at TheActivatorBook.com/Resources.

EXAMPLE QUESTIONS

Goals

What outcome do you want?

What do you want to focus on?

What is your goal?

What do you want to achieve?

What problem are you trying to solve?

What is your top priority?

What is one thing you want to change?

Options

What options are available to achieve your goal(s)?

What are the possible ways to reach your goal(s)?

What have you done before in similar situations?

What have you not tried?

What is missing?

Obstacles

What might get in the way?

What is missing?

What obstacles might you face with this option?

What are the potential hurdles?

Is this a sustainable idea?

Can you build a plan for this?

Does this option need a "Plan B?"

Action Planning

What are the most viable options?

What needs to be the first step?

What is your step-by-step plan?

What resources will you need?

When do you plan to accomplish each step?

What roadblocks might you encounter?

Leverage Accountability

What will you have accomplished by this time next week?

How will you stick to your commitment to accomplishing this goal?

How would you like me to hold you accountable?

When would you like me to follow up with you?

What can I do to support your efforts?

How do you plan to measure your change?

GIVING CONSTRUCTIVE FEEDBACK

Giving constructive feedback may be one of the most uncomfortable tasks of a leader. I have talked to many leaders who have admitted to giving as little feedback as possible due to the anxiety this kind of interaction produces. On the flip side, there are also some leaders who do not hesitate to give constructive feedback and often do it hastily and without skill, resulting in distrust by the employee.

When you have developed a coaching relationship with a person and have effectively used the skills of listening and questioning, you will find you have laid a solid foundation to enable effective feedback. Here are the six steps of giving effective constructive feedback.

1. *Plan how you will give feedback.* I have experienced, and perhaps you have too, what happens when a leader doesn't think through or prepare for a constructive feedback conversation. When we become uncomfortable or nervous, we can easily freeze up and not know what to say. When we experience stress and anxiety, it is easy to forget what we intended to say. Before giving feedback, take a few minutes to think about and then write one or two statements you want to communicate to the other person.

2. *Ask for permission.* You want to create a safe environment for people to experience constructive feedback. Remember that the person's brain is going to default to "threat mode" if they do not feel safe or feel attacked. You will have a much better outcome if you do everything possible to reduce the threat the person is feeling.

A great way to reduce the threat response is to ask the person, "Can I give you some feedback about...?" Ninety-nine percent of the time, the person is going to say, "Yes." When you ask for permission first, you are showing respect to the person while also allowing them to gain a sense of ownership in the process. This is a persuasion technique that allows a person to express willingness and commitment to something. When people express this, they are more willing to listen, accept, and take action on it. Why? Because they have verbally stated that they want to hear it. Dr. Robert Cialdini, author of Influence: The Psychology of Persuasion, calls this principle "Consistency,"[2] because most of us desire to have consistency between our words and our actions.

"What if they say no?" If this happens simply say, "Okay, I understand that now isn't a good time. Let's plan to connect tomorrow to discuss." Make it a point to connect with the person the next day and ask, "Is this a good time to provide you with some feedback?"

3. *State your intent.* Before jumping in with your feedback statement, tell the person why you are giving them feedback. When we receive feedback from someone, we ask ourselves *"Why is this person giving me constructive feedback?"* We can easily answer this question negatively due to our brain's instinctual attunement to threat and survival. It can be easy to think that a person is giving you constructive feedback because they think it makes them feel superior. Perhaps we might think that this person doesn't like us anymore or they are mad at us. Stating your intent upfront heads this off and answers the question. Your direct report will likely be more open to your feedback.

To do this well, you need to make a statement that helps them understand that the feedback will benefit them. Here are a few examples of what you could say.

- ⚡ *"I want to give you some feedback to help you perform at a higher level next time."*

- ⚡ *"I want to give you my thoughts on this; it could help you knock this project out of the park."*

- ⚡ *"I want to give you some feedback that will provide some new insights that I believe you will find helpful."*

- ⚡ *"My hope is that you achieve at the highest level possible, so I wanted to give you some feedback that could help."*

4. Deliver the feedback message quickly and concisely. You've been there both as an adult and as a teenager. The dreaded "sermon." This is when the person giving you constructive feedback won't stop telling you what you did wrong or how to fix it. They go into preacher mode and go on and on about your mistake. A person will raise their emotional resistance walls after hearing their failure more than once. Keep your feedback message short and to the point. Then quietly allow the person to respond. If it feels right, ask questions to gain clarity about the situation.

5. Coach the change. The old management perspective would say that now is the time to tell the employee how to change. However, good coaching leaders take a different road and ask the employee what he or she can do to change or move in the necessary direction. This approach helps you activate their brain since you are handing over the responsibility to them to determine how they will reach the goal of change or improved performance.

6. Express your confidence in the person. Everyone needs to feel encouraged, especially when receiving constructive feedback. Take time to tell your employees that you have confidence in their abilities to make the change. You can state this directly or connect the employee's strengths with the new direction they are taking.

CHALLENGING

Think about a time when you were challenged by someone to improve in some way. I would imagine your experience was a lot like mine; very uncomfortable. But I was glad the person cared enough to give it to me. When you were challenged, it likely made you aware that your current level of focus, energy, orbehavior was lacking, and someone—whether it was a teacher, coach, supervisor, parent, spouse, or a friend — saw that you were not living up to your potential. It is this insight, and perhaps a message that accompanied it, that prompted you to make a change.

Supervisors who use a coaching approach look for opportunities to challenge employees. They look for places to help people "up their game." Managers, who act as coaches, refuse to allow people to be mediocre. To challenge people, you have to get them to think better, deeper, and sometimes broader than they normally would. Our brains are wired to take the easy route. Why? Because its most important function is to keep us alive. This means it tries to expend the least amount of energy and calories possible. Your brain will find shortcuts and use tried-and-true methods of thinking and processing. In fact, this is where habits help us. Habits are processes we have put into place that become automatic and so efficient that it requires little energy from our brain.

You can use brain science to help your direct reports think better and solve problems more effectively. Neuroscience studies provide many insights into how we can Activate optimal brain function that leads to better thinking and behavior. Management researchers, Adam Waytz and Malia Mason discovered two major functions of the brain that are responsible for processing information and creating ideas. They called these two functions the "default network" and the "control network." The default network of the brain leads to creativity and innovation as it activates during times when a person is not focused on one thought. Waytz and Mason describe this function as the ability of our brain to "transcend" the current situation and environment.[3] We can daydream, imagine, and see ourselves in a different place. This ability fosters imagination and ideas.

The "control network," on the other hand, is the brain function that focuses on the present and the current environment or immediate need at hand. This thinking mode uses calculations, analysis, and detail orientation to completed tasks that require deeper thought and contemplation. Work that requires the control network (deeper processing) can be greatly hindered by environmental distracters like email, meetings, phone calls, as well as unimportant administrative duties that cause mental distraction or anxiety.

Leaders can activate employee brains by challenging the thinking patterns and decisions people make to accomplish their work. An example of this is challenging employees regarding the "network" they are using. When you see an employee that needs to be spending time using their Control Network to gain focus for deeper work, challenge him/her through questions or messages that help them to become aware of their behavior and make them rethink how they approach their work.

You might ask, "How are you working toward being more efficient with your work?" or "What do you believe is standing in your way of achieving your goal more quickly?" Have a discussion and then share your knowledge with the intention to partner together to create a plan of action. Here are a few ideas to implement into your coaching that will foster your ability to challenge people.

1. *Work structure and calendar.* Challenge employees to determine when and how they can employ their control and default networks to generate better results. Contrary to popular belief, there is a place and time for multi-tasking.

2. *Make room for intentional "default network" time.*

✦ Coach people on how to use their brain optimally. This includes taking breaks for recuperation, eating to fuel the brain, movement during the day, and rest.

✦ Coach people on how to structure and budget their time (calendars) to allocate dedicated time for both default and control network-oriented tasks.

✦ Create workplace boundaries or schedules that foster time for default work, collaboration and idea generation, and control work—encouraging time for focus, quiet, and no interruptions

3. *Push back.* This is a variation of feedback as it gives you an opportunity to share your own thoughts, ideas, and perspectives. You may want to begin your statement with something like, "Please allow me to push back for a moment." Pushing back encourages the person being coached to step out of his or her own mindset and think about other perspectives.

4. *Ask two key challenging questions.*

✦ *"How are you giving your best in this situation?"*

✦ *"If you were to challenge yourself, what would you do?"*

These questions allow the person being coached to think, process, and arrive at the person's own conclusion about his or her actions and behavior. Using questions as a means to challenge is an effective approach for people who are naturally more defensive or guarded.

5. *Create discomfort.* Our human nature seeks comfort, but we don't progress or learn when we are in a constant state of comfort. To help a person grow, we must guide them to a place of discomfort. There are many ways to achieve this, such as

stretching a person's goals, asking them to do something differently, or assigning a special assignment to them.

6. *Ask for a stretch goal.* Research on goal setting and performance tells us that when employees set goals for themselves, they usually set the goal at a level for which they feel confident in their ability to achieve. This makes sense because we all want to reach our goals and avoid adverse consequences or embarrassment. Stretch goals create some healthy stress that produces motivation to give more focus and effort. When the employee achieves this kind of goal, confidence increases, growth occurs, and satisfaction soars.

7. *Accelerate their timeline.* Accelerating the timeline involves moving the target date up for either taking action or achieving a goal. It is easy to say that you'll take action on this problem next week. Yet, in using the skill of challenge, you may want to ask, "What stands in your way of taking action today?" Similar to the substance of the goals themselves, people set target dates for their goals that are comfortable and can be reached with plenty of time to spare. Managers who want to accelerate a person's achievement timeline may make a statement such as, "I bet you can accomplish this goal within the next 30 days. What would it mean to reach your goal quicker?"

Great managers don't sit back and expect high performance to happen, nor do they command better performance with overbearing communication or threats. Instead, they use the skill of challenging to take their thinking, behavior, and performance to a higher level.

COMMENDING

Using words and phrases "Great job" and "Way to go" to praise people has limited impact. Commending is more powerful than the standard praise and recognition statements leaders make because it seeks to communicate to a person their value more so than their success. Commending is a great way to boost the confidence of your people while helping them feel genuinely appreciated.

One of the greatest desires we possess is to be valued by others. We all want people to value our gifts, uniqueness, and contributions we make to our team or organization. Appreciating people by saying "Thank you" and recognizing good work is important. Commending, however, goes a step further as it identifies and appreciates a person's character strengths. Below are three principles for commending employees.

Value the person more than the action. We all want to be valued for who we are more than for what we do. Managers can easily fall into the trap of recognizing or praising only behaviors. Look for opportunities to highlight their character, talent, and intent.

Point out their unique contributions. Express the strengths and contributions of each employee as you communicate with them. Be specific about what each person brings to the team, organization, and even the world. Identifying their uniqueness can stimulate confidence and the feeling of being valued and appreciated.

Point out the impact of their behavior. Be intentional about going beyond complimenting the person's behavior to highlight the impact it has had on others. This will provide the employee with feedback, reinforce the high-performing behavior, and communicate how the person impacts others.

Here are some sample commendation statements that utilize these three principles.

⚡ *"Your presentation was excellent. I believe the group now has a clear understanding of the project. We are fortunate to have you on our team!"*

⚡ *"Thank you for your hard work on this. You have a great work ethic."*

⚡ *"The way you handled that conflict showed your patience and commitment to helping every person on this team succeed."*

When you recognize an employee in this way, you activate the brain, increase oxytocin, and boost dopamine levels. And people leave the meeting inspired with more energy, motivation to pursue their goals, and a greater desire to engage in their work.

COACHING TIPS

Here are few coaching tips that will help you to become even more effective.

Shoot straight with questions – When asked tough questions, answer them directly and honestly.

Put the responsibility for thought back on the employees – Do not get sucked into the question, "What should I do?" or "What do I need to do in this situation?" Ask questions so employees learn to think on their own and not depend on you.

Restate what you heard – This will help you ensure your full understanding of the situation and will help the employee gain clarity of the situation as they hear it restated.

Help employees rethink what is possible – Employees often come to their supervisor with an "I'm at the end of my rope" mindset. They frequently believe they are out of options and ideas. Use a positive mindset, statements, questions, and ideas to spark new thoughts and ideas.

Be calm and confident – During a crisis, employees want to see a leader who is calm and confident. Your attitude and approach will help the team feel similarly.

Help them learn to reframe any situation – Psychological research tells us that we can mentally reframe any situation. We can take a problem and view it as a challenge instead. This kind of mindset shift can help a person move away from an attitude of failure and victimhood to one of control and success. Use questions and statements that help the employee see how something difficult can be turned into something good.

Ask the employee to take notes and recap the meeting – Use this technique when you want a specific outcome or behavior to occur after the meeting. This will ensure both parties are on the same page and that the employee understands your expectations.

End meetings with a reference to purpose or meaning – State the meaning and purpose of the employee's work. Help them see how their work will make a significant impact.

Be approachable and accessible – If you are not accessible or approachable for assistance and feedback, employees will not feel like they can count on you for support. Look for ways to demonstrate behaviors that simultaneously support these attributes.

Relax and be real – Being relaxed will put employees at ease. Communicate to your employees that you don't expect perfection from them, but that you expect them to do their best.

Help people see their roles – Communicate to your employees the strengths you see in them and how they can best use these strengths to help the team.

Let the employee be right – Do not always have the answer. Help employees discover their own answers and get credit for them.

Celebrate – Whenever possible, find ways to celebrate the accomplishments of individuals and the team. Look for even the smallest excuses to celebrate.

COACHING EMPLOYEE GROWTH AND DEVELOPMENT

I often hear leaders complain about the lack of motivation people have around self-development. I hear statements like, "I don't know why our people complain about not having opportunities or budget for development when there are plenty of free options available to them." Or they might say, "Why do I always have to be the one prompting people to grow their professional skills? Why won't they take initiative themselves?"

I spent many years asking these same questions myself. When I finally thought through the dynamic, I began to understand the two key barriers that stood in the way of an employee taking initiative to develop themselves.

The first barrier is that they believe their development is the responsibility of the employer rather than their own. This is a fallacy that plagues many workplace cultures. A person who believes it's the company's responsibility to develop them will often wait for the company to find budget dollars and then invite them to a program or training session. When this doesn't happen, many people will do nothing except complain that their company doesn't develop them. While companies should be investing in the development of their people, each person needs to learn to be self-directed. When a company provides opportunities and resources, it is a bonus.

A second barrier is a lack of support for being self-directed in their development. The support of a manager isn't always needed, but it can be a motivation catalyst for a person to grow. The most powerful development tool is coaching. When a leader uses a coaching approach to ask an employee about their goals, aspirations, professional direction, and development, it prompts self-directed action. It activates the brain of the employee to think, plan, and take action for growth.

Very few people want to become stagnant professionally. Although some don't care to progress to a role with higher responsibility, most people rarely want to stay the same. Great managers try to develop employees by coaching them on their career passions, motivations, vision, and goals. Managers can help employees connect the dots between each of these areas, and show them the path to better themselves and achieve in a way that brings them satisfaction.

STRATEGIC COACHING CONVERSATIONS

There are times when you want to be more strategic in your coaching because you need to guide the person toward an outcome that is beneficial to both of you. These "strategic conversations" are coaching opportunities focused on general topics that are important to the employee's work and career. It's strategic because you initiate the conversation after careful thought for how you will provide guidance.

These conversations rely on questions to prompt employees to think about who they want to be and what they want to accomplish. They connect the "who" and the "what" to the "how." The "how" is the action that needs to take place. Strategic coaching conversations activate the employee's brain and provide focus and energy. Here are some examples of strategic conversations you can have with employees.

Development Conversations - A conversation that explores growth, development needs, strengths, and any weaknesses that need to be developed or managed.

Stay Conversations - A conversation to discuss what the employee likes about their work, why they stay, and what they don't like, along with what might prompt their desire to leave and how to manage them.

Reconciliation - A conversation that is focused on caring for an employee after a disagreement or conflict—between the two of you, or between the employee and one of their coworkers. This conversation is focused on checking the person's emotional state and determining what needs to happen for the person to move forward in a positive and productive way.

Performance - A conversation that is focused on helping the employee improve their level of performance. The employee doesn't have to be a low-performer. This strategic conversation can also be used for those who are performing well, but you believe they aren't performing close to their potential. Explore their engagement and the level of challenge their current goals are providing for them. Then help them create an action plan.

Career Planning - A conversation that explores the employee's career goals and professional dreams. Help them create a career development plan and align it with their intrinsic values and desires. Help them make connections between what they do now and how it can help them achieve their career goals.

Activators ask questions, listen, explore ideas, and provide resources. They use the GOAL model to guide the conversation and help employees set clear goals, collaborate to create options and determine how to handle obstacles, and prompt employees to move ideas out of their heads and onto paper in the form of an action plan.

Finally, Activators provide accountability by setting a date for follow-ups to check progress and provide further support. The My Development Plan (MDP) worksheet is a template you and your employees can use to document goals, action steps, behaviors, timeline, and resources related to the person's development agenda. Download a free MDP worksheet at TheActivatorBook.com/Resources.

Coaching is not only a method to manage performance and engagement, it is a leadership skill that builds a standard for interaction within your culture. When people experience the power of coaching, they will naturally want to use the same conversational approach in their communication and collaboration with others. Overtime this will form a solid foundation for a culture of excellence.

BRAIN ACTIVATION - COACHING TACTICS

 Listen deeply. Make listening your top priority during interactions with others. Listen with your eyes, face, voice, and body language.

 Create a threat response plan. When you determine something is causing a threat, make a plan of action for how you can help reduce the perception of threat. Then take action.

Lead with questions. Take an inquiry approach to interactions and conversations so you can increase employee discovery, thinking, analysis, responsibility, and growth.

 Make feedback safe. Reduce the level of threat by planning and executing feedback by first writing the feedback statement, asking for permission to give feedback, and then stating your intention for giving it.

 Challenge to accelerate. When you see that an employee isn't setting their goals or personal expectations high enough, bring it to their attention. Use positive inquiry or statements to express your confidence in their ability to achieve at a higher level or more quickly.

 Initiate on-ramping. When someone new joins the team, have a special extended meeting to discuss your management style and expectations. Let them know how you support and coach performance and feedback.

 Inform of accountability measures. Be open and precise about accountability measures. Make consequences and rewards clear, timely, and fair.

 Engage in scenario planning. Challenge your employees to imagine different scenarios. Then ask how they will handle the situation?

 Utilize visualization. Ask employees to visualize a situation or outcome. Ask them to imagine seeing it, feeling it (emotions), and experiencing it (actions) in a successful way.

 Lead strategic coaching conversations. Strategic conversations are focused on general topics that are critical to overall success at work and for the person's career. Topics include:

⚡ Development - Continual professional growth.

⚡ Stay (loyalty) - Discover what employees love about their work and why they stay.

⚡ Reconciliation - Managing conflict and disagreements.

⚡ Performance - Application of the person's potential now and into the future.

⚡ Career Planning - Career goals and professional dreams, aligned with their development plan.

 Feed-forward. Tell employees what you believe they will do well in the future or how they will succeed on a project or task.

 Highlight strengths. Tell employees the strengths you see in them. Look for and commend each person's unique character and skill strengths.

 Point to progress. Tell people when you see the progress they have made toward a goal, a project, personal growth, or any outcome they are pursuing.

 Acknowledge stagnation. Use questions to call out a lack of progress, motivation, or engagement that you see on the part of an employee. You can use questions like, "Is this still important to you?" "What progress have you made in the last two weeks?" and "How can I help you regain your momentum?"

 Reframe failures. Help people find nuggets of learning with mistakes and failures. Ask people, "What did you learn from this experience?" or "What will you do differently next time you face a similar situation?"

 Invite ideas. Ask people what ideas or input they have on a decision or challenge.

 Ask for commitment. Don't expect commitment; ask for it. You can ask questions like, "Can I get your commitment to making this happen by next Friday?" or "Will you commit to making this change?"

 Resource people. Ask employees what resources they need to support their success. Resources may include people, connections, time, money, information, and training, among many other things.

 Show appreciation. Take time to say "Thank you" for effort and commitment. Writing a note to a person is often more powerful than email or verbal expression.

 Conduct experimentation. Frame change as an opportunity to experiment, learn, and try new things. Use a discovery and test approach for new processes, products, services, and ideas.

Appoint a leader. Increase a person's sense of status and responsibility by giving them a responsibility that requires them to lead people and achieve a goal or outcome.

Build intelligence and confidence. Ask people their thoughts and ideas on challenges. Acknowledge their ideas as smart, creative, innovative, or perceptive.

Encourage well-being. Help people monitor their stress levels and work-life integration. Encourage rest breaks during the day and days off from work.

Deemphasize extrinsic rewards. While it may be tempting to emphasize incentives and bonus programs, remember that these programs can decrease intrinsic motivation. Place emphasis on helping people align their values with their work and team goals.

Teach brain optimization. Encourage and commend healthy brain habits. Highlight brain-draining activities that could harm performance and help people avoid them.

CHAPTER 8
CULTURING

SETTING AND UPHOLDING STANDARDS OF EXCELLENCE

There is a popular psychology experiment that many people apply to workplace culture. The experiment was called, "The 5 Monkeys." It showed that monkeys who are sprayed with water (as a punishment) while climbing a ladder to reach a group of hanging bananas would cease trying to climb the ladder. Then when other monkeys enter the cage, they would not attempt to climb the ladder to retrieve the bananas, even though they had never been sprayed with water.

The application of the research, according to those who use the story, is that our workplace is similar to that of the monkey's culture. It suggests that people stop trying things when they know others have been punished for trying similar things in the past. This experiment has been used for years to help people understand the phenomenon and avoid the "We've always done it this way" mindset. You can do an internet search and find many articles and videos that describe the study. But there's one major problem with this experiment. It never happened!

Over time, this story has taken on a life of its own. Although it was attributed to a 1967 Gordon R. Stephenson journal article, the research project never used bananas, a ladder, nor a blast of water.[1] How could so many people believe, much less use, a story that is inaccurate and say it's a scientific experiment? It's not because they enjoy lying or want to manipulate you. Rather, it's because they have been influenced by others to believe it is a true story. This is what can happen when communication is embellished to aid a point or when multiple ideas (experiments in this case) get combined. Early communicators of this story likely confused Stephenson's experiment with the primate research of Wolfgang Kohler in the 1920s, who used bananas and ladders. This highlights a common human phenomenon related to sharing information. We believe something is factual without evidence of its validity. The speed at which this happens seems to be increasing in our current society that is driven by social media and the proliferation of internet communication full of unverified information.

Oddly enough, the example of this study (that never happened), and how it proliferated is evidence for the principle that the story was trying to prove in the first place. Our social environment is a powerful system of ideas, beliefs, and behaviors. Your workplace culture is not a set of value statements placed on the wall or a pretty picture with a caption about teamwork in a conference room. Your culture is a dynamic and a constantly evolving system of feelings, beliefs, and expectations.

Culture is defined by people in different ways. One of the most ambiguous definitions states that culture is your organization's personality. Other vague definitions describe culture as the "character" of your company or the "feel" of your organization.

The culture of a team or organization is an amalgamation of the brain processes and behaviors of every person within the culture. Every person contributes thoughts, experience, perspective, and behaviors. But that's not all there is to a culture.

A large ingredient to this mix is the social component that is made up of the standards, expectations, threats, and reinforcements that take place every day within the group of people within the culture. With this in mind, a thoughtful and organized definition of culture within the workplace is this: *a culture is made up of a group's values, beliefs, and behaviors that provide a compass for social alignment, consistency, and success.*

A healthy culture can become a competitive advantage in the marketplace and serve to be the factor that distinguishes you from your competitors. This is why Peter Drucker once said, "Culture eats strategy for breakfast." Healthy culture attracts talent. People want to be a part of a healthy culture because it has the potential to bring out the best in them. Many elements of culture that we experience every day are driven by the values, beliefs, and behaviors of people.

⚡ *Leadership* - how leaders communicate and interact with people in light of the mission, vision, and values

⚡ *Management* - processes and policies that delegate tasks and empower people to get work completed

⚡ *People* - interactions, skills, personalities, styles, and beliefs of people who compose the culture

⚡ *Resources* - tools, objects, and technology that support people to get work accomplished

⚡ *Compensation* - pay and incentives provided to people in exchange for their work

⚡ *Opportunity* - continual learning, development, and advancement opportunities

According to a study by the National Bureau of Economic Research, 85% of Chief Executive Officers (CEOs) and Chief Financial Officers (CFOs) say unethical behavior is a direct result of an unhealthy culture.[2] The study also found that nine out of ten financial chiefs believe that companies can increase their performance by improving the culture. A struggling or negative environment often has deficits in at least one of the elements listed above, which can hinder people's willingness to give their best at work and support their teammates.

Sadly, a survey by Achievers found that only 45% of employees believe their leadership is committed to improving culture.[3] Couple this with what CEOs and CFOs believe, and you find a large discrepancy between leadership beliefs, and what they are actually doing. The most effective leaders understand that culture shaping is a critical part of their responsibility and take action to build a great place to work.

I use the word culturing, because culture is not a destination. It is an ongoing process that requires intention and constant work to create an environment where everyone can thrive. Leaders cannot dictate culture. Many leaders create a set of ideals and expectations for what they want their culture to be, and then they communicate their vision to the team hoping they will "buy-in" to it. Many then wonder, why nobody is taking it seriously and improvement isn't happening. This approach backfires on them or is accepted with little enthusiasm and commitment.

People are naturally skeptical and often rebel against complying with standards or changes they don't understand or haven't participated in choosing. People want to feel a sense of ownership for their culture. Leaders who use older motivation tactics including reinforcements and punishments often find that people will initially align their behaviors with the leader's culture script, but over time, their allegiance to the standards fade. Entitlement and fear often become the result of bribes and punishment, not commitment.

Activators take a different approach to leading people. The activation approach seeks to lead people to a deeper level of engagement with their work and their environment.

THE 3 LEVELS OF ENGAGEMENT

We can categorize people into three different levels of engagement. Each category is associated with a depth of commitment represented by behavior that shows that level of commitment.

MEMBER

The first level is the member; this is the shallowest. Members usually comply with the standards, directions, and goals of the team, but with little commitment. These people do what they are told and adhere to expectations in exchange for employment and compensation.

It's important to understand that members can demonstrate various engaged or disengaged behaviors, from noncompliance and undermining behaviors all the way to fulfilling job duties with a sense of duty. In other words, members can fall along the continuum from apathetic to moderately engaged. The reason I put them at the "member" level is because they have chosen to be on the team. You may have members of your team who hate their job. For some, it's obvious. These are the people who can easily be identified as disengaged. Then there are other members who don't hate their job that are also disengaged. These people actually look like they are happy and will rate themselves as "satisfied," on engagement surveys. Just like Cal in chapter 3, these employees have decided that they will comply with expectations for a fair exchange such as a paycheck or job security. These people are not engaged. They are giving just enough to get by and contribute minimally to the goals of your team. There is a big difference between the member level and the next level.

OWNER

The Owner level is marked by having a sense of responsibility for the culture, behaviors, and outcomes the team or group creates. Owners have made a conscious and logical decision to participate in the creation of the culture and take responsibility for the team's outcomes. Most owners don't have a leadership title, yet they take a leadership role. They lead through their attitude, words, and actions by supporting the direction of leadership and giving their best.

The Owner level is where we hope to get everyone on the team. Owners want to exert influence and control to gain the outcomes they feel is best for themselves and the team. Owners have a great sense of pride in their team and will always give extra effort to achieve team goals that align with their personal values. While we want to get everyone to the ownership level of engagement, there are a few who will go to an even deeper level, turbocharging your culture.

ACTIVIST

Activists are engaged at the deepest level possible. The Activist's commitment to the culture is not just rational; it is emotional. The biggest distinguishing factor between the Owner and the Activist is that activists have an emotional commitment that drives a fanatical focus on the mission and outcomes of the team. This level of engagement can often be described as obsessive.

Activists must be careful not to become workaholics. The team's goals are also a central part of the Activist's identity. They are highly dedicated to their work and their colleagues, and they take great pride in what they do.

An activist's commitment runs so deep that if they aren't careful, they can be perceived as being blinded by emotions and allegiance. An example of this would be a person who has become an activist for a political party or sports team. These people are deeply ego-invested, and they see the success of their work as a direct reflection of themselves. Sense activists are often emotional about their affiliation, they must be careful that they don't become irrational.

MEMBER	OWNER	ACTIVIST
DISENGAGED	MODERATELY ENGAGED	FULLY ENGAGED	DEEPLY ENGAGED

Activists are evangelists for their organization. They identify with the purpose of the work being done. They want to talk about the impact of their organization not because it's a reflection on them, but because they want to bring others onboard with their beliefs, experience, and mission. They believe so deeply in what they are committed to that they want as many other people as possible to be a part of the movement.

Another distinguishing characteristic of activists is their focus on the bigger picture. They are committed to making everyone around them more successful, not just themselves. Their commitment guides them to think with a long-term perspective so the organization outlives them. Activists only feel successful when the group achieves success.

There was a point in time when Michael Jordan was an owner of the culture of the Chicago Bulls. He was engaged and performed well; people around him also performed well. But it wasn't until he became completely dedicated to making everyone around him better that the team took a leap forward and became a basketball dynasty, winning multiple world championships.

MEMBER	OWNER	ACTIVIST
Compliance-Based	Rational-Based	Emotional-Based
Belonging	Influencing	Creating Change
Individual Benefits	Team Benefits	Outsider Benefits
Role Success	Collaboration	Empowerment/Growth
Individual Goals	Team Goals	Mission
Comfort	Work for Desired Outcomes	Sacrifice for a Cause
Short-term Perspective	Long-term Perspective	Legacy
Enjoyment/Happiness	Impact	Significant Change

When you understand the different levels of engagement, you are better equipped to facilitate and coach movement to a deeper level. Imagine if every person on your team was an owner or an activist. If that were the case, you would have a highly motivated and deeply engaged group of people that contribute to a winning culture.

So how do we get people to this level of engagement? It's not by telling them to or incentivizing them to do it. People don't become owners and activists through rewards, free stuff, or any other extrinsic manipulations. They may look like it in the short-term, but they won't in the long-term.

You'll just have to keep feeding their motivation through extrinsic reward that satiate and fatigue, losing power over time. It's a game you can't win. Instead, Activators understand the power of the environment and seek to build and strengthen this external mechanism of motivation.

FRAME YOUR CULTURE

The FRAMEwork method (introduced in Chapter 5) is a simple way to assess, monitor, and build a work culture. Although I provided a brief overview of the FRAME model earlier, let's take a deeper look at how you can use this method to build a world-class culture.

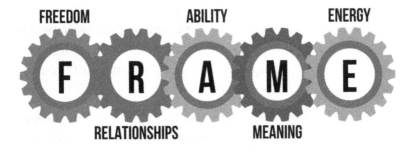

FREEDOM

Our globalized and virtualized world is demanding the use of an autonomous and flexible paradigm of work and leadership. Surveys continue to show an increase in the value people place on work schedule flexibility, work-life balance, work mobility, and choice. We are seeing the will and needs of people being expressed in their demands for greater autonomy and trust. Edward Deci and Richard Ryan believe so strongly in the need for autonomy that they say it is one of the "innate psychological nutriments that are essential for ongoing psychological growth, integrity, and wellbeing."[4] Autonomy is a core requirement for a person to develop and thrive. They validated the prevalence of this belief in the workplace with a study they conducted with researcher Paul Baard within an investment banking organization.[5] They found that managers who provided more "autonomy support": gave freedom, choice, and opportunity: had employees who reported higher levels of job satisfaction and work performance.

The doctoral dissertation I completed many years ago was based on a study I conducted investigating the impact of freedom on employees involved in a rigorous workplace training program.[6] In this program they not only had to demonstrate they had acquired knowledge of how an automatic mail sorting machine worked, they also had to demonstrate that they could trouble-shoot it and then fix the problem. High achievement in the program meant that a person had to demonstrate high levels of proficiency on both knowledge and procedural performance tests.

After following more than a hundred employees through this three-week training program and measuring motivation and performance, autonomy stood out as an intriguingly powerful factor in predicting the success of an employee in the program. Employees who reported feeling more autonomous also felt more confident in their ability to learn and achieve. They also exhibited higher levels of self-managed behavior and higher-quality motivation, ultimately resulting in higher levels of knowledge and procedural performance.

These studies, among many others, show the impact that freedom has on factors that support a healthy culture such as a person's feelings of control, self-management, intrinsic motivation, competence, and confidence in their ability to succeed.

Workplaces where people feel a sense of freedom and autonomy also produce employees who take greater responsibility for their work, leading to higher levels of creativity, innovation, and quality.

Freedom, however, is more than flexibility. It requires a style of leadership that many managers struggle to provide. It's not independence. Freedom is felt when someone believes they have choices for how they complete their work or how they achieve their work goals. Daniel Pink's analysis of the research on autonomy in the workplace led him to suggest four essential areas that when freedom is given, intrinsic motivation skyrockets.[7]

Task - Giving people freedom to choose the tasks and projects they work on. Give people time to work on passion projects, innovate, and apply their creativity.

Time - Giving people some freedom over their time and flexibility for how they get their work done. Move away from an 8 a.m. to 5 p.m., "putting your time in" paradigm to a goal performance paradigm as a way to measure work performance.

Technique - Giving people some freedom over how they do their work and achieve their performance goals. Maintain goal standards and delivery deadlines while giving flexibility to how an employee achieves the goal.

Team - Giving people some freedom to choose their colleagues. Allow input on who works together on projects, teams, and committees together.

A preeminent characteristic of an Activator is her passion to trust and empower others. This requires the release of control and becoming vulnerable to failures on the part of your employees. At the same time, it reminds us of the importance of coaching performance and cultivating an environment that supports the success of every person. Freedom takes root and thrives in a culture where everyone is committed to helping their colleagues succeed. Here are some more specific ideas that you can apply to your workplace to strengthen freedom.

- Allow employees to create individual goals when possible.
- Allow teams to create their goals whenever possible.
- Encourage employees to create professional development goals and action plans.
- Build a flexible work environment.
- Focus on goal achievement, not how many hours are worked.
- Give employees control over how they reach goals.
- Refuse to micromanage.
- Use language that connotes freedom and autonomy.
- Eliminate unnecessary policies and rules.
- Allow virtual or mobile work when possible.
- Facilitate the expression of differing perspectives and ideas within the group.
- Promote and support employees' work-life balance.

RELATIONSHIPS

Research has shown supportive relationships are a crucial component to employee commitment and achievement on the job. A positive relationship is also a major factor leading to our personal fulfillment in all aspects of our lives, including work. Motivation can be supported and increased when people feel a strong sense of belonging, when they feel needed, and when they have a solid support system. This kind of support also leads a person to feel a sense of responsibility to help others, thus reinforcing the desire to nurture valued relationships.

Think about the groups of people you have enjoyed being around; those with whom you felt a sense of care, belonging, need, and support—friends, a football team, an orchestra, a church or synagogue, sorority or any one of a million associations. My point is that none of these groups have a name that creates culture. The people, and the environment they built together, created the culture you want to be a part of. And I'm betting you were compelled to contribute to it because of the positive impact it had on you.

THE SOCIAL BRAIN

A mounting body of neuroscience research is revealing an interesting dynamic that happens between people. As we spend more time with others, our brains begin to sync together. This has been known for decades, through physiological studies related to hormonal changes.

More recently, neuroscience has discovered that our brains communicate with one another in ways we can't see or measure. Scientists refer to this as the "Social Brain." An example of this is our innate ability to read and provide unconscious responses to social cues. Our brain can perceive the smallest of facial changes and body movements to make interpretations for how to behave in socially appropriate ways.

Brain scans have been able to connect social cues with certain brain functions. A part of the brain known as the fusiform gyrus, located at the bottom of your brain, interprets even the smallest of facial differences in structure and expressions. The fusiform gyrus likely works with the amygdala, found deep inside the temporal portion of the brain, to process emotion-based signals. The amygdala's job is to interpret and guide reactions that are emotion-based.

Studies show that people who have damage to this area have a difficult time differentiating facial and body language that indicate extreme emotions such as fear. Together these areas of the brain help us determine whether someone is familiar and trusted. They also help us determine what their emotional state is and therefore predict how they will behave. This is quite handy for survival and also aids in our social interactions. We have many other neural networks that are dedicated to processing and interpreting voice tone, touch, and smell, among many other functions that are socially important.

Have you ever wondered why yawning is contagious? This is your brain's mirroring system at work. Neuroscientists have identified neurons that primarily function to mirror the behaviors of others.[8] These "mirror neurons" are another mechanism our brain uses to help us relate well with other humans. Mirror neurons are likely involved in smiling when others smile, laughing when others laugh, and when we unconsciously change our body positioning and language to match the body language of others.

Scientists believe we are only scratching the surface in understanding how our brains communicate with each other. What is most important to note about the social brain is that we have the opportunity to increase our interpersonal and professional success when we prioritize awareness and relationship building with employees and co-workers. The science is clear; relationships are at the heart of teamwork and collaboration.

PERFORMANCE SUPPORT

In 2012, Google set out to build the perfect team. They gathered data analysts and researchers inside the company and began collecting data from thousands of employees across 180 teams.[9] They looked at a multitude of variables, including intelligence, skills, experience, emotional intelligence, and task speed. After crunching the data, they found that there was no profile that would determine a perfect employee team member or performer.

Instead, they found that high performance for both teams and individuals could only be predicted by the people around them: their team. Two variables were found to be the most important for the highest performing teams. First, the team was composed of people who had built and managed strong relationship bonds; they called this "social sensitivity."

Secondly, the team created an environment of equal and safe communication. Harvard Business School professor Amy Edmondson calls this "Psychological Safety": a team climate characterized by interpersonal trust and mutual respect.[10] Teams with high psychological safety have members who are willing to take risks around their coworkers. They believe that their teammates won't embarrass or punish them for making a mistake, offering an idea, or asking a question.

Psychological safety is also influenced by situational influences, like changes that disrupt the way we work. David Rock, the author of *Your Brain at Work*, developed the SCARF model as a tool to help leaders understand how certain situations can threaten people. The model helps leaders assess and take action to address the five social rewards and threats that are important to brain function.[11]

STATUS - A person's social need for esteem and respect.

CERTAINTY - A person's need to know and predict what will happen next. Familiar situations give the brain comfort, while unpredictable situations produce discomfort and anxiety.

AUTONOMY - A person's sense of control over events and situations, and opportunity for choice. Choice is a major component for creating a sense of control and autonomy.

RELATEDNESS - The level of safety and comfort we feel with other humans. We are hard-wired to judge people's intention to either harm us or help us.

FAIRNESS - The perception of fair exchange between people and if people are treated justly.

According to Rock, each of these social components activates one of two responses in the brain. The "primary reward" response is triggered when a person perceives an event as supportive of one of the SCARF elements. The "primary threat" response is triggered in the brain when a domain is perceived to be negative, adverse, or a threat to current beliefs.

One interesting and practical example of the primary reward versus threat is fairness in the workplace. Numerous studies reveal the sensitivity people have related to their perception of fairness. Humans are keenly aware of the interaction of the people around them and make comparisons to their own interactions with others. When discrepancies are perceived, it can cause a threat response.

The way in which relationships create psychological safety and help us mitigate threats at work aren't just a "nice to have" in our organization. Rather, they are a key driver of optimal brain function and chemistry that supports engagement and performance. It turns out that Aristotle was right when he said, "The whole is greater than the sum of its parts."

Strategies that can help you enable and encourage relationships, and that also demonstrate your care and value for each person, include:

- ✦ Get to know every employee on a personal level.

- ✦ Encourage all team members to connect with each other on a deeper level than work (e.g., know about each other's hobbies, interests, passions, families, etc.)

- ✦ Help employees to understand the strengths of their teammates.

- ✦ Facilitate team-building activities to help team members learn how to collaborate.

- ✦ Facilitate team discussions about team goals, processes, standards, expectations, and accountability.

- ✦ Recognize the work of each team member publicly so everyone is aware of the contributions of other team members.

- ✦ Hold "off-site" meetings for employees to plan together, share ideas, and build camaraderie.

- ✦ Have one-on-one conversations with each employee at least twice a month.

- ✦ Discover the desires and values of each employee.

- ✦ Commend team members when they support and help each other.

- ✦ Celebrate both individual and team accomplishments.

⚡ Model mature friendship and apply healthy conflict-resolution strategies.

ABILITY

Our sense of ability is rooted in our need to learn, grow, achieve, and master challenges. Growth and mastery occur when we are challenged by a goal, take action, and then achieve it. Once you have reached your goal, you feel satisfied and ready to take on the next challenge.

This is the reason why gaming is such a popular hobby for both children and adults. The gaming industry has thrived in recent years because they have created games with progressive mastery. In fact, playing video games is one of the most addictive activities for humans.

The progressive mastery process results in a neurological response that involves a stream of hormone and neurotransmitters being released that activates multiple areas of the brain. Dopamine, adrenaline, serotonin, oxytocin, norepinephrine, testosterone, and others aid our body and the brain's ability to guide us through a process toward achieving our goals. But this focused achievement state only occurs when we are in an environment that supports the strengthening of our abilities.

When a person feels overwhelmed by their goals, lacks support in reaching them, or feels a sense of failure, they release the stress hormone cortisol into their bloodstream. Cortisol has its benefits when it is used briefly by the body. But cortisol causes major problems when it circulates in our bodies for a long period of time. It can contribute to high blood sugar, high cholesterol levels, lower immune function, weight gain, and heart disease. Cortisol also suppresses executive brain functions like critical thinking and decision-making and hinders the release of dopamine and oxytocin, which are important for connecting with others and feeling happy and fulfilled in our work.

When people feel like they can reach a goal or perform a task well, they have what Stanford University professor, Albert Bandura, calls self-efficacy. A person's confidence grows as their sense of ability strengthens. According to Bandura,

People who have a strong belief in their capabilities think, feel, and behave differently from those who have doubts about their capabilities. People who doubt their capabilities shy away from difficult tasks. They have low aspirations and weak commitments to the goals they choose to pursue. Failure wrecks their motivation. They give up quickly in the face of difficulties and are slow to recover their confidence following failure or setbacks. [12]

A study by management professors Henry Sauerman and Wesley Cohen investigated the work habits of thousands of engineers and scientists.[13] They found that those who sought out intellectually challenging work were more intrinsically motivated and performed better on the job. The data also showed that the scientists and engineers who were intrinsically motivated to work on intellectually challenging tasks filed significantly more patents than their counterparts who reported being motivated by money. Environments that challenge us to get out of our comfort zones and solve problems support our natural brain wiring, resulting in greater intrinsic motivation and often in better performance and achievement.

Great leaders look to activate people through an appropriate level of challenge. They co-create goals and action plans with employees to create a sense of ownership while monitoring the level of difficulty so that it fosters growth and confidence. They understand that goals that are too easy don't stimulate or engage the brain.

Likewise, goals that are too difficult cause a threat response that hinders motivation and performance. Managing this balance is a challenge for any leader. Coaching can help you strike the balance as you set expectations, monitor performance, give feedback, and establish accountability.

Finally, Activators support the ability of people by facilitating collaboration among colleagues, providing the appropriate resources and training and development opportunities. Here are a few ideas for strengthening an employee's sense of Ability.

- ⚡ Provide the best onboarding and training experience possible.

- ⚡ Provide employees with the resources they need to do their job effectively.

- ⚡ Define the results and outcomes employees are responsible for delivering.

- ⚡ Communicate performance expectations clearly.

- ⚡ Give employees timely feedback for work performed, covering both process and results.

- ⚡ Acknowledge and celebrate each employee's achievements.

- ⚡ Look for areas to coach employees and give constructive feedback respectfully.

- ⚡ Help employees challenge themselves and stretch their goals.

- ⚡ Model and reinforce positive communication (words, tone, facial expressions, and body language) during meetings and conversations with employees.

MEANING

The question of how people find or create meaning on the job has been pondered for many years. Dr. Steven Reiss' exhaustive research that sought to discover what makes life worth living provides us with the most accurate understanding. The sixteen Basic Desires is a practical way to think about what we personally define as "meaningful." You can help the people you lead connect the dots between their desires (values/motivators) and their work tasks, as well as the organization's goals. Facilitating strategic conversations with employees that help them create alignment between their basic desires and their work is critical for helping them feel a sense of satisfaction and purpose at work.

There is another level of meaning we need to address. It is a group's shared sense of meaning. We want people to find a sense of personal meaningfulness at work, but great teams have created a purpose for their collaboration. This happens when team members commit to working towards common goals that are aligned with each individual's sense of purpose. Activators can cultivate shared meaning within a group of people by helping the team set expectations and standards in several key areas.

Mission. Effective leaders work with their team to create a shared mission or purpose, which defines and clarifies why the team exists and what they are there to do as a part of a larger team. Activators help people create a "line-of-sight" between their individual work tasks all the way to the mission of the organization. To do this, you must help people connect the dots: like tasks, goals, team goals, and team missions: along the pathway toward the organization's mission.

171

Standard Operating Procedure. Activators work with their teams to create a set of values for how work is done. If the mission is the "what," standard operating procedure is the "how." Activators communication performance, standards, and behavior expectations in one-on-one conversations and in-group discussions. While it would be, near impossible to document every standard that a culture has—values, attitudes, unwritten rules, treatment, interactions, conflict management, etc.—it is important to speak up when unwritten rules and the positive norms of the team are broken or disregarded. In doing so, you can maintain the strength of the culture and uphold a high standard of behavior.

Impact. Impact is focused on the shared mission a team has to make a particular impact on something larger than the business or organization. In some organizations, this is made explicit in the mission statement, but in many, it is not. There is great value in differentiating a team's contribution to the organizational mission and the team's impact beyond the organization. Activators help their team see how they contribute to the world in a positive way. Communicate the impact often and when possible, allow people to see the impact it is making first-hand.

Storytelling. Humans have used storytelling since the dawn of time to communicate important information. While we all love a good story, the field of neuroscience has revealed that hearing one actually stimulates our brain. Stories activate the parts of our brain that aid attention, focus, pleasure, and memory. Paul Zak, founding director of the Center for Neuroeconomics Studies and author of *Trust Factor: The Science of Creating High-Performance Companies*, found that character-driven stories cause oxytocin levels to rise in listeners, leading to higher levels of trust and cooperation. Zak explains, "Experiments show that character-driven stories with emotional content result in a better understanding of the key points a speaker is communicating and enables better recall of the points several weeks later."[14]

Telling brain-activating stories isn't hard, but it is helpful to know the attributes of a story that makes it connect and stick in people's minds. Kindra Hall suggests the following four key components in her book, *Stories That Stick*.[15]

- ⚡ **Identifiable Characters.** Introduce a character people will care about and with whom they can connect. Describe characters so an image can form in the listener's brain.

- ⚡ **Authentic Emotion.** Convey the emotion felt by the character or that is caused by the situation. According to Hall, "It is through emotion that the story receiver experiences empathy with the story. No emotion means no empathy. No empathy means reduced impact of the message."

- ⚡ **A Significant Moment.** Explain a point in time, circumstances, or setting. Take the story down to a specific situation. Help people understand and visualize the context and environment that is creating the emotion of the experience. The story I told in the last chapter about Coach King is an example of this principle. Rather than telling you that he was a referee at my game, I told you about the significant moment when I made a tackle and heard him say, "Nice tackle." Then I looked up and discovered it was Coach King. Telling you this part of the story emphasizes an important emotional moment that helped you feel my surprise. It helps you connect with the story and then remember the idea I was communicating.

- ⚡ **Specific Details.** Give details that help people visualize and find themselves in the story. Hall explains, "Specific details engage the imagination of the audience. This component pulls the audience deeper into the world of the story, a world that, if done right, will look and feel familiar."

Stories can help people find a sense of meaning. You can make a vision and mission come alive when you use a story to communicate it. Using a story to set a standard prompts people to take greater ownership and live up to expectations. When you are encouraging your team to keep moving forward through challenge or change, a story can be the activator of cooperation, resilience, and grit.

A fight. Let's be honest, a nicely phrased mission statement, or a set of values with a creative image placed on the wall isn't energizing or engaging. People want a cause to fight for and to become an activist in a movement. David Burkus, organizational effectiveness researcher and author of *Pick a Fight* says, "The simplest and most effective way to build a high-performing team that stays together, despite the stress of the challenge, is to get that team working together against a common enemy. In other words, pick a fight!"[16]

Activators articulate the battle that the team is fighting and the reason why it should be fought. They define the enemy and invite people to join a movement toward something better, right, or just. They look for ways to connect the battle to what people find meaningful. According to Burkus, "People don't want to join a company; they want to join a crusade." When teams find meaning in working (and fighting) together, they become more cohesive and engage with energy and passion. As you seek to strengthen a sense of meaning on the part of your employees, here are a few ideas to consider putting into place.

⚡ Help employees to understand their intrinsic values, desires, and what is meaningful to them.

⚡ Encourage employees to create a personal mission.

⚡ Help employees develop a team mission that aligns with the company's mission.

⚡ Help employees to bridge the connection between the team's mission and their personal ones.

⚡ Communicate the impact the team and each individual makes on the company and the world.

⚡ Recognize each employee's unique contribution to the team and to furthering the organization's goals.

⚡ Communicate the team's mission and vision often and with meaningful stories.

ENERGY

The energy of an environment is contagious. An environment with positive energy breeds more of that energy. Employees who have positive energy support the positivity of their coworkers. Just one person can significantly alter another person's neurological chemistry for better or worse. And it only takes a second for this to occur.

This happens through what scientists call a process of "interpersonal limbic regulation." Our internal chemistry can be altered by another person's behavior, affecting our hormone levels, neurochemistry, sleep rhythms, immune functions, and cardiovascular functions. One person's behavior can cause a production of oxytocin, resulting in greater trust; in the same way, a person who brings poor energy and mood can alter the mood and chemistry of other people around them. Daniel

Goleman, Richard Boyatzis, and Annie McKee call this phenomenon the "open-loop system" since our limbic system is so responsive to external sources.[17]

This open-loop system design helps us survive in situations where people can be a support for each other to boost emotion, positive energy, immune system, and arousal when it is needed for fighting or reproduction. But the open-loop nature leaves us more vulnerable when we are surrounded by people with negative behavior, mood, and energy. A study of 70 work teams by Caroline Bartel and Richard Saavedra at the University of Michigan found that employees who worked together in teams began sharing the same moods within two hours.[18]

These moods were found to be both positive and negative in nature and spread with consistent amplitude. When good energy is present in an environment, it results in the following culture characteristics.

- ⚡ Fun/Playfulness
- ⚡ Creativity
- ⚡ Positive attitudes
- ⚡ Less complaining
- ⚡ Hero rather than victim mentality
- ⚡ Happiness
- ⚡ Cooperation
- ⚡ Collaboration
- ⚡ Relaxed at appropriate times
- ⚡ Focused at appropriate times
- ⚡ Passionate Engagement

↯   Health conflict

↯   Leveraged strengths

↯   Resilience in the face of adversity

↯   Challenge-seeking rather than challenge-avoiding

The emotional energy each person brings to the environment is significant. But the energy of the leader has the most impact since they hold the most power in the group and are typically the most visible. Employees take their emotional cues from their leaders as they guide what attitudes and behaviors are acceptable and desired.

This is the reason that leaders are uniquely positioned to be Activators of people. They are the tone-setters for the culture and set the thermostat for energy. When activators consistently and dependably bring a positive emotional energy to the environment, it becomes a force that guides people to bring the best of themselves to their teammates and their work.

A few years ago, I was facilitating a leadership workshop in Fort Smith, Arkansas. The participants car-pooled from surrounding cities early that morning so we could begin the program by 9:00 a.m. Shortly after everyone arrived, one of the participants began to panic as she searched for her keys. She was the driver of one of the company's carpool vans and had responsibility for the keys, which she had lost.

Everyone in the room started helping her look for them. A few seconds later she exclaimed, "Oh no, I accidentally flushed them down the toilet!" She then explained to the group that she remembered briefly seeing something odd being flushed. She was mortified, but also angry with herself since those were the only keys that could drive her and four others back to Little Rock.

She called her supervisor, who was the senior vice president of her division, and humbly explained the situation with profuse apologies. Her boss told her he would take care of it and that she should carry on with the workshop.

A few hours later, as I was facilitating a discussion with the group, a gentleman poked his head into the doorway and said, "Did someone flush some keys?" The group laughed, but at the same time they were surprised to see that Rodney, the department's vice president, had driven the keys there himself. It didn't take long for us all to find out why.

Rodney asked if he could address the group. Of course, I allowed him to proceed. He stood in front of the group and began telling them about how much a certain manager and her team had done over the years to help and sometimes save him from difficult situations. He said it was about time he got the opportunity to do something to save her. Then he asked her to join him in front of the group with her team. "I have made the effort to bring you the keys along with a special keychain so you don't lose this set." He then pulled the set of keys out of a bag to reveal that the keys had a small toilet plunger attached to them. The group roared with laughter.

I was impressed with the fact that he had not only delivered the keys himself, but that he took the time to stop at a hardware store to buy a small plunger, drilled a hole in the handle, and attached it. I was most impressed by this leader's commitment to setting a positive energy tone for the culture. He could have chosen to be upset or frustrated by the mistake. He could have complained about the loss of productivity. He could have used the situation as leverage in their relationship. Instead, he turned it into an opportunity to bring levity, humor, fun, and show appreciation to an employee. He took an opportunity that could have caused negative energy and created a memorable moment that nobody in that room will ever forget.

Here are a few more ideas that can help you bring positive and healthy energy to your team.

- ⚡ Develop your positive energy and model it to others.

- ⚡ Smile.

- ⚡ Don't accept toxic behaviors from people with negative energy.

- ⚡ Teach people how mood and energy impact others.

- ⚡ Encourage a healthy lifestyle, which may include balanced nutrition, regular exercise, and personal development.

- ⚡ Provide healthy snacks and lunches during meetings and special events.

- ⚡ Schedule frequent breaks during meetings.

- ⚡ Encourage healthy work-life integration.

- ⚡ Celebrate and recognize individual and team achievements.

- ⚡ Commend and appreciate employees who display positive energy.

AVOIDING CULTURE SLIPPAGE

The organizations that I have worked with over the years that seem to have the highest sense of urgency to improve their culture are the ones that have told me that their culture was slipping. I often hear statements similar to the following:

"As we have grown, our culture has changed."

"We have lost the culture we set out to create."

"We aren't who we used to be."

"We've become so busy that we've lost sight of our values."

These are statements of culture slippage. There are times when moving the culture is more difficult and takes more focus and time. But building and maintaining a great culture always takes intention. This is why I call it culturing. It's an ongoing process.

As a leader, if you put culture on the back burner, it will slip. But remember that Activators don't dictate culture. You must invite people in and empower them to be a part of the culturing process. Activators ask everyone to shape the culture they want to be a part of. As you do this and you demonstrate the virtues of an Activator, you will develop activators around you and who will help continuously shape a winning culture.

BRAIN ACTIVATION - CULTURING TACTICS

 Model and Encourage Psychologically Safe Behaviors. Facilitate the balance of communication within a group. Ask those who have been quiet to provide input. Commend people who demonstrate emotionally intelligent behaviors (self-awareness, social awareness, self-management, and relationship management). Praise and appreciate people who take emotional risk when they speak up or share their thoughts and ideas.

 Mitigate Threats. Identify the potential threats that employees may be facing using Rock's SCARF model (Status, Certainty, Autonomy, Relatedness, and Fairness). Take action to reduce the level of threat for each area. Ask people (one-on-one or group) what they worry about or what has the potential to stand in the way of their progress and success at work. You may also want to ask about the things that they dislike or that annoy them at work.

 Enable Job Crafting. Work with employees to build their job role and tasks around their strengths and intrinsic values. There will be boundaries and tasks that can't be altered, but where it is possible, allow employees to make adjustments and changes for how their work is completed.

 Provide Flexibility. Build a "results-oriented" work culture where people focus on achieving and reaching work goals and help others to do the same, rather than on policing who comes and goes at certain times. Implement fair and equitable guidelines where everyone understands how the system works and people can hold themselves accountable. Consider giving time off to employees for recovery after achieving a big goal or completing an intensive project.

 Encourage Good Health and Well-being. Facilitate sharing of health and well-being goals and resources among your employees. Commend progress and accomplishments. Be sure to bring healthy lunches, snacks, and drinks to the office when you are treating the team. Be an example of healthy living.

Be a Super-Connector. Be on the lookout for ways to connect people. This could be as simple as facilitating ice-breaker questions and activities at the beginning of meetings or appointing two employees to work together on a project. Consider how to connect your employees with people outside of your team who can serve as helpful resources or network connections.

 Harness Defining Moments. After a difficult or stressful situation has occurred, process the experience with your team. Talk about what was done well and what could be improved when the situation occurs again. Remind the team that their behaviors during difficult times define the culture.

 Demonstrate Fairness. Evaluate how you treat employees, including your positive behaviors, to ensure some employees aren't getting special treatment. Evaluate how much time you spend with each employee, whom you meet with more often, whom you talk to more often, whom you go to lunch with, and to whom you delegate high-profile tasks. Make behavior changes to create fairness for all your employees.

 Master Meetings. Think of your meetings as an opportunity to boost energy and motivation. Unfortunately, most meetings do the opposite. Start meetings positively. Have an agenda and a defined outcome. Then shorten one-hour meetings to 45 minutes, allowing time for transition and reducing the stress of moving from one meeting to the next. If possible, reduce meetings to 30 minutes.

Hold Challenge Sessions. Create special meetings to challenge your team with a question, issue, problem, or decision related to the work of the team or organization. Communicate the challenge and then facilitate brainstorming and collaboration on ideas. Ask for different perspectives. Appoint a "Devil's Advocate" to test ideas and perspectives.

 Set the Language Standard. Your language cultivates one of two brain modes: Threat or Thrive. Be an example of positive language and power words that cultivate confidence, trust, and openness among people. Speak up against language that cultivates distrust, fear, and divisiveness.

 Use a Team Mantra. Using a simple phrase or mantra often builds sheathing (insulation) between neurons in your brain. This sheathing facilitates memory, quick processing, automaticity, and familiarity. Building a mantra is a good way to remind ourselves of our work standards or goals.

There is no right way to create one, just think about what will help your team keep focused on the high standard of excellence you want to maintain. Google has used "Do the right thing!" Apple used "Think Different" during the years of its greatest growth and innovation. GE used "Unyielding Integrity, Commitment to Performance, and Thirst for Change" when they were making major changes in the quality of their products. Dyson uses "Solving problems others ignore."

Facilitate Cooperation Over Competition. Competition can hinder cooperation. Be sure that individual goals don't take precedence over or impede team goals. Create and encourage interactions where each member's work and goals support their coworkers' achievements.

 Ask for Help. Be an example of collaboration by asking people for help. Don't be a "know-it-all" or a "do-it-all" person. Leverage the strengths of others by asking for their help. This not only builds connection, it builds a culture of openness, humility, and cooperation.

 Tell Stories. Stories engage the parts of our brains that process humor, emotion, visualization, memory, and creativity. Use stories to engage people's brains, maintain attention, and build credibility and trust while also communicating the standards of the culture.

 Make Vacations a Big Deal. Commend people when they take vacations and time off. Vacations help the brain rest, recuperate, and restore motivation; but only when they are completely disconnected from work duties.

 End Traditional Performance Evaluations. Nobody likes them and the evidence shows they are ineffective. Create an alternative process such as quarterly or monthly coaching sessions that focus on expectations, goals, feedback, and development.

 Don't Force Rank Employees. This process can be effective in rare situations, but it creates an environment of threat and competition that hinders optimal brain function. If you determine a rating is needed, then rate employees against the expectations and goals of their role rather than against each other.

 Leverage Fun and Humor. Take time to find fun and humor in the workplace. Allow appropriate joking. Play games. Go off-site for a meeting.

 Gamify Work. Increase energy and engagement by harnessing the brain's desire for challenge, mastery, reward, recognition, novelty, and fun by creating games that move people toward individual and team goals. Games include streak tracking, dashboards, leader boards, mission trackers, checklists, scoreboards, trivia games, and many others. There are numerous resources and applications on the market that can help you create and implement gamification.

 Facilitate Limbic Regulation. When you see a person or group is becoming frustrated, call for a break. Allow people to take time to cool down and get their brain chemistry back into normal range.

 Take a Field Trip. Visit an organization in a different industry to see how they succeed. Then facilitate a discussion with your team about what they experienced and learned during the trip. If the conversation doesn't naturally shift toward applying the principles, then ask, "What did they do successfully that we could apply to our work?" Another variation of a field trip is to secret shop a competitor. Then reconvene and discuss what was discovered.

Stand-Up Meetings. Hold meetings in a location that requires the group to stand or at least not sit in a comfortable conference or office chair. It is healthier than sitting as it promotes heathy blood flow and muscle movement. You will also create a sense of urgency that is usually lost during sitting meetings.

Prime the Brain. When you send an email about a meeting or a calendar invite, use power words to prime people for the meeting. For example, you might say, "Be thinking about how we will approach this new economic challenge. I would like everyone to bring at least one idea to the table."

Mindfulness Meetings. Start meetings with a mindfulness tactic. Take three minutes to allow people to express what they are happy about or what they are grateful for that day. You can also ask the group to reflect on one of the following areas: recent accomplishments, who they appreciate, and how they plan to be successful that day.

Help People Study Their Brain. Challenge people to study their own brains. Encourage them to monitor their sleep patterns and the best time of the day for certain tasks like deep and shallow work. Other brain functions to monitor are best time of the day for energy, best foods for energy and thinking, caffeine intake and crashes, fatigue, and rest breaks.

Get to the Why? When an employee shows interest, passion, or motivation for a task or outcome, ask what they find meaningful about it. When you're coaching and have covered "The What" (goal) and "The How" (the action plan), ask about "The Why" (why this is important).

 Create Standard Operating Procedures. Facilitate a discussion with your team about the standards they want to set for themselves. You can ask questions like, "What are acceptable ways to manage conflict of disagreement?" "What are unacceptable ways to handle conflict or disagreement?" "What standards or rules do we want to have for ourselves related to how we collaborate and communicate together when serving a client?" Document these standards. Communicate them often. Finally, hold people accountable to them when they behave outside of the standard.

 Appoint Experts. Create a list of knowledge, skills, or ideas that you would like to add to your team's capability. Delegate one of the items to each person on your team. Ask them to research and learn about the subject to become the team's resident expert. You can ask them to give a presentation or mini-training on the topic to the team. Also, refer to the expertise of your employees during team discussions to get their perspective based on their research.

 Empower Passion Projects. Allow people to spend 5-10% of their time at work focusing on a challenge, idea, innovation, or research that they have interest in and that would be helpful to the organization or team.

CHAPTER 9
ACTIVATOR DEVELOPMENT

You don't become a great leader by accumulating years of experience, titles, degrees, certifications, or awards. The true measure of effective leadership is found in how you facilitate the success of others. Ernest Hemingway once said, "There is nothing noble in being superior to your fellow man; true nobility is being superior to your former self." Being an Activator is the process of facilitating greatness in the people around you. It requires an internal strength that must be maintained. A strength that lies beyond authority and power.

You have likely either read the children's book or heard the story of *How Full is Your Bucket?* by Tom Rath and Mary Reck-Meyer. The story is about a boy who learns that he has a figurative invisible bucket that gets filled or depleted by interactions with others. As the story progresses, he is able to see that everyone has a bucket and that he has the power to put drops in it or dip them out. After a while, he discovers that each time he treats someone kindly: dripping water into that person's bucket: it automatically drips more water into his own bucket.

This is a simple story with a powerful message to people of all ages. As leaders, we can glean an additional principle from this story. We can't always rely on others to fill our bucket, so we must take consistent action to do things that fill our own bucket. In doing so, we don't run dry and render ourselves unable to give to others. You can't give from what you don't have.

Activators continually develop themselves in ways that create strength, character, skill, and mindset so they can facilitate these same qualities in the people they lead. Here are several ways to continually grow and develop yourself.

Self-Activate. Apply the principles of activation to yourself. Get a deep understanding of your basic intrinsic desires, and then seek activities and work that support them.

Construct Your Reality. Take control of your environment and reality. Refuse to blame others or circumstances and take action to build a FRAME environment. Think about and take action to build a life and work environment for yourself that provides high levels of support for freedom, relationships, ability, meaning, and energy.

Sleep. Get plenty of it.

Rest. Take breaks throughout the day to let your brain reenergize.

Drink Plenty of Water. Drink at least 64 ounces of water every day. Start your day with at least 16 ounces to hydrate your brain.

Eat for Brain Power. Eat healthy foods that are low in sugar and give your brain the nutrients and carbohydrates it needs to function optimally.

Create a Winning Morning Ritual. Your brain loves predictability and accomplishment. Set your morning up to make small wins quickly and create achievement momentum for the day. Examples include making your bed, flossing, exercising, reading, writing, enjoying time with family, eating a healthy break-fast, and anything that makes you feel good about accomplishing early.

Reflect. Take time before going to sleep at night to reflect upon and appreciate the events of the day. What went well, what didn't go well, what you learned from it, and how you want to be different the next day?

Physical Fitness. The health of your body has a significant impact on the health of your brain, and vice versa. When you work on both, it provides a positive cycle of health that gives support to both elements of your energy.

Study Yourself. Determine the areas you would like to learn about yourself, take action to assess them, and then leverage or develop accordingly. For instance, you might take time to chart your best sleep hours: when you go to bed and when you wake up. Determine the best time to exercise. You might want to study your food intake to determine what foods work best for you to lose weight, feel better, or reduce body inflammation.

Manage Stress. Determine the best ways to manage your stress, both acute (short-term) and chronic (continual). Meditation, focused breathing, walks, and conversations with friends are examples of acute stress management tactics. Exercise, days off, sabbaticals, coaching, and counseling are examples of tactics to manage chronic stress.

Mind Your Mindset. Check your mindset often. Using Carol Dweck's mindset model, reflect on the past week and ask yourself if your thinking and behavior were growth-oriented or fixed. Growth orientation is when you believe you have control over your outcomes and growth. Fixed orientation is when you feel your outcomes are out of your control, you didn't seek to learn or grow, and you blame others when things go wrong. Take action to become growth-oriented.

Personal Mission/Vision. Create a personal mission or purpose statement. You may also want to create one that is geared to your leadership and career. Make it as short and concise as possible so you can memorize and say it to yourself.

Goals. Create personal and professional goals along with an action plan. Feel free to use the My Development Plan (MDP) worksheet that you can download for free at www.TheActivatorBook.com/Resources. Review each goal and your progress at least once a week, if not daily.

Laugh. Be with friends. Spend time with friends. Talk about challenges, enjoy fun activities, and laugh together. The dopamine hit you get from this kind of interaction makes you feel better and live longer.

Be Kind to Yourself. Leaders can be hard on themselves. Often, harder on themselves than on others. Remember that balance and rest are essential elements to your performance and growth. Give yourself permission to take care of yourself. Monitor your self-talk and work on replacing negative language with positive.

Get Organized. Your brain needs organization. It functions on structure and clarity. Take time to organize the things in your life that need more stability and predictability—especially in those areas you've been avoiding. Build processes that help you maintain your organization. There are many applications and physical resources (like office supplies) that can help. Eliminate unnecessary things or activities in your life. Examples of areas to organize include personal records, finances, insurance documents, legal documents, filing cabinet, desk drawer, desktop, books, garage, vehicle, tools, kitchen, pantry, and don't forget that closet.

Reward Yourself. Determine two main ways to reward yourself. One is small and the other is large. Use small rewards on a daily basis. This could be taking a walk, eating a snack you like, or playing a game on your phone. Use the large reward only when you achieve a larger goal. This could be going to a restaurant you love, a day at the spa, or shopping for a gift for yourself.

Continue Learning and Growing. You are doing it now. Way to go! Make continual learning and growth a lifestyle.

Find a Mentor. Build a relationship with someone you admire and can help you learn from their experiences. Don't approach someone you don't know or barely know and ask them to mentor you. You don't have to ask to be mentored. Just create a relationship. Ask for time to get their advice and guidance as needed. Don't use obligatory monthly meetings. As the relationship flourishes, express your appreciation to the person for helping and mentoring you.

Get a Coach. While mentors provide guidance based on their experience and background, a coach can be someone who supports you, and holds you accountable for your growth and development. A coach will help you clarify your goals, create action plans, and help accelerate you toward achievement.

We have the luxury to access volumes of ideas, articles, documents, books, and courses on leadership. In fact, it's become quite overwhelming for leaders to know where to start. I want to encourage you to focus on applying the three core Activator skills (Connecting, Coaching, Culturing), and apply the Brain Activation Tactics that fit the situations you find yourself in for the next three months. Read the core skills chapters in this book several times. Go to TheActivatorBook.com and take advantage of all the resources available to you. And take time each day to think about how you can better connect, coach, and culture your employees.

Becoming an Activator is about investing in something beyond yourself. It's becoming stronger and healthier. Activation is living larger by pursuing a potential that is bigger than just your personal achievement. It is understanding that if we only focus on our own success, we miss out on a greater success. Being an Activator is choosing who we want to be, how we want to live, and deciding how we will show up each day for others. When you Activate people, you unleash the greatness that they hold within themselves and you bring out their true potential making our world a better place. You have what it takes and now you know a proven method for how to do it. Now, go light people up!

APENDIX

THE 16 BASIC DESIRES REFERENCE GUIDE

The 16 Basic Desires discovered by Steven Reiss is the first empirically derived, standardized set of human needs, values, and motives. It is a proven taxonomy of human needs identified through a process of factor analysis (mathematical congruence of goals) of data ascertained from a diverse sample of people. The Reiss Motivation Profile (RMP) was created to provide people with a valid and reliable measurement of the intensity of all sixteen desires. Numerous peer-reviewed studies have been conducted to confirm construct validity, reliability, concurrent validity, and criterion validity. You can find additional information related to the research supporting the desires at www.DrJasonJones.com/RMP.

Each person has a unique combination of desires which fall somewhere along a continuum between the two poles of strong and weak. This approach honors individual differences and uniqueness among people as it can produce billions of potential combinations of motivation profiles and explain unique personalities.

Desires are intrinsic motivators because they are at the root of our most basic needs and values. They are ends-oriented, not means-oriented (extrinsic in nature). For example, money is means-oriented because it is a motivator that has no inherent value. People are motivated to gain money (digits in an account) not for the money, but for what the money can help them achieve or buy (the ends). Ends-oriented motivators include a feeling of tranquility (low anxiety) or curiosity (learning for enjoyment). A person may be motivated to make money, but the true ends motivation is likely to fulfill a high need or two: like saving for future retirement (tranquility) and purchasing a new course (curiosity): which are intrinsic in nature.

People pay attention and are more sensitive to stimuli that are relevant to satisfying their desires. People pay little attention or ignore stimuli that aren't related to their stronger and weaker desires. For example, people who have a stronger desire for vengeance can easily perceive behaviors of others to be provocations or insults. Someone with a strong desire for idealism will be highly attuned to situations where people need help or support.

You can learn more about using the Reiss Motivation Profile® for personal, team, or organizational development by visiting www.DrJasonJones.com/RMP

A description of each of the 16 desires is listed below. Further information for study can be found in Steven's Reiss's book, *Who Am I: The 16 Basic Desires.*

Acceptance – Acceptance is the desire to be accepted and to avoid criticism. If strong, a person greatly desires approval. They can also lack self-confidence and have feelings of insecurity. They are hurt by criticisms and constructive feedback if not provided with care and support.

People who have a weak desire for acceptance don't care about what other people think about them. They have a high level of confidence and aren't swayed by the opinions of others. They handle criticism and constructive feedback well and take it less personally.

Beauty – The desire for an aesthetically pleasing environment. People who have a strong desire for beauty find great satisfaction in a physical environment that is beautiful, artful, and pleasing to the senses. They are motivated by making their environments or themselves aesthetically pleasing in some way. They also enjoy spending time in places and environments that they consider visually or aurally pleasing.

People who have a weak desire for beauty do not care about the aesthetics of an environment. They may find certain attempts for beautification to be off-putting. These people enjoy plain or simply decorated places. They usually have little desire to make things look nicer, beautify an area, or spend their time admiring art, landscaping, fashion, or anything that has been designed for beauty.

Curiosity – The desire to learn and understand. People with a strong need for curiosity embrace cognition, thinking, and gaining knowledge. They like to create, test, and teach others about new ideas. People who have strong curiosity typically have a broad range of interests. They may have found a variety of areas to focus on and have vast levels of expertise.

People with weak curiosity dislike exerting cognitive energy. An intellectual lifestyle seems boring to them. They value work or activity more than thought and contemplation. They don't enjoy reading, studying, watching documentaries, or engaging in intellectual conversations. They often view those who are strong in curiosity negatively.

Eating – The desire to eat food. People with a strong desire to eat find great joy in the activity. While eating is a physiological need, in the context of intrinsic motivation this desire is psychological in nature. They will gain great satisfaction from the act of eating the foods they love and often find enjoyment in making food for others to enjoy.

People with a weak desire for eating typically have a small appetite, sometimes forgetting to eat. They do not gain any intrinsic satisfaction from eating and may find taking time to eat to be a waste of time.

Honor – The desire to behave with high character. Those with a strong desire for honor are loyal to the expectations and norms of the groups, teams, and society to which they belong. They find great satisfaction when they follow the rules and meet expectations that others have for their actions. They focus their behaviors on being dependable, honorable, and principled.

People who have a weak desire for honor do not conform to what others want for them. They typically are more rebellious and may not adhere to the norms of a group, team, or society. They gain great satisfaction from being different, strong-willed, unconventional, and unique.

Family – The desire to raise children and spend time with family. People with a strong desire for family enjoy the duties of parenting and caring for the needs of their family. They have a strong value for family life and find great satisfaction in nurturing others.

People who have a weak desire for family do not gain great internal satisfaction from parenting duties. They do not find great meaning in having children and find a sense of purpose and satisfaction in other activities.

The level of desire does not determine how good a parent is, but it can be an influencing variable. Some people with a strong desire for family have not had kids and can find alternative methods to gain satisfaction for their need to nurture and care for others. Some people who have children have a weak desire for family but prioritize their duty and maintain their responsibilities.

Idealism – The desire to improve society. People who have a strong desire for idealism find great satisfaction in helping people. They are interested in current world events and seek to bring awareness to others about humanitarian problems and injustices. They find great satisfaction through involvement in philanthropic causes and enjoy volunteer work to help others.

People with a weak desire for idealism are more focused on their own life events and issues more than on the society around them. They typically pay little attention to problems plaguing society and do not sacrifice their own time to volunteer for activities that help people or communities.

Independence - The desire to rely on oneself. People who have a strong desire for independence are self-reliant. They gain satisfaction from individual work and achievements. They don't like to rely on other people, and are often viewed as lone wolves.

People with a weak desire for independence like to rely on and support others. They enjoy being a part of a team and value building rapport and trust with others. Those who have a weak desire for independence gain more enjoyment from achieving with others rather than alone.

Order – The desire to be clean and organized. People with a strong desire for order gain great satisfaction from being organized, tidy, and punctual. They often enjoy the process of organization, and revel in their accomplishments that involved working to clean, detail, and structure. People with a strong need for order dislike ambiguity and can be frustrated when their environment isn't predictable or organized.

People who have a weak desire for order become annoyed by structure. They may believe time spent organizing and cleaning is a waste of time. They gain satisfaction in being spontaneous and flexible.

Physical Activity - The desire for physical movement and exercise. People with a strong desire for physical activity create personal satisfaction and vitality through vigorous activity. They take great pride in staying fit and healthy. Those with a strong desire for physical activity can grow frustrated when in environments that are inactive, indoors, and don't allow for physical movement.

People with a weak desire for physical activity enjoy sedentary activities and gain great satisfaction from leisure and relaxation. They are typically less secure in their physical capabilities, which can lead to a desire to avoid activities with which they have little experience.

Power – The desire to lead and influence others. People with a strong desire for power naturally take charge in situations involving other people. They find deep satisfaction and enjoyment in making decisions and influencing outcomes. They are often assertive and outcome-focused.

People who have a weak desire for power find great satisfaction through supporting and following others. They don't like leadership roles or having to make decisions on their own that impact many people. They are often easy-going and nonassertive.

Saving – The desire to conserve and collect. People with a strong desire for saving find security in accumulating, collecting, and even hoarding items. Some may also find great satisfaction in saving money, being frugal, or not letting anything go to waste.

People with a weak desire for saving find little to no value in saving, collecting, or conserving items. They tend to use things quickly with no thought of conservation. Some may even be wasteful. Others might be extravagant spenders. They are typically bothered by the actions of people who demonstrate a strong desire to save.

Social Contact – The desire to be with people. People who have a strong desire for social contact find great internal satisfaction from being around other people. They are often very social and have refined social skills. If their desire for social contact is not met, they may feel lonely and highly dissatisfied.

People who have a weak desire for social contact find satisfaction in solitude. They typically dislike large gatherings and prefer to have a smaller group of friends. They can easily become annoyed by being in contact with too many people.

Status – The desire for prestige and social standing. People who have a strong desire for status find great satisfaction in feeling significant or "somebody." They tend to pursue money, titles, fame, or items that are symbols of status, such as cars, houses, and clothing. They also seek to associate with other people they believe have status.

People who have a weak desire for status find satisfaction in maintaining equality among people and are unimpressed by people with money, titles, authority, and status symbols. They maintain a strong belief that people should not be judged by their wealth, family, career, or job title.

Tranquility – The desire to avoid stress and anxiety. People who have a strong desire for tranquility find great internal satisfaction when they feel safe and secure. They find great value in reducing risk and want to avoid anxious experiences. They seek relaxation and security.

People with weak tranquility find great satisfaction in taking risks. They tolerate stress well and can easily become bored with security and safety. They often seek activities considered risky and manage ambiguity and uncertainty better than those who have a moderate or strong desire for tranquility.

Vengeance – The desire for vindication. People who have a strong desire for vengeance find great satisfaction from getting even with people. They are more confrontational than most and enjoy competition. They will also stand up for others while demanding or creating justice. This person may be perceived as more aggressive than most.

People who have a weak desire for vengeance avoid conflicts and confrontations. Although they may have the skills and desire at times to confront someone or stand up for someone, their first instinct is to avoid competition and cooperate. They value peace, mercy, and forgiveness.

ACKNOWLEDGEMENTS

Writing a book isn't a solo journey. It took a year to write, but two decades to formulate. Over these years, I have spoken to thousands of people who have allowed me to share my ideas and graciously provided me with honest feedback.

This book is only possible because of the hard work that so many have given to their study and research. It would be impossible to thank all the people who have influenced me over the years. Some of them proceeded me in life and some I have never met, yet their thinking and writing has enhanced my knowledge and understanding.

Throughout my professional career I have known, followed, and collaborated with some truly outstanding people; many of them have taught, led, helped, and supported me over the years. If you've spent any significant time with me, then I have learned from you. You are amazing and I thank you for sharing your life with me.

I'm fortunate to have had several long-time mentors in my life. They have truly been my Activators. Much of who I am today is because of these people. Ben Glover, Barbara Greene, David Mitchell, Michael Roach, and Paul Stoltz have been significant encouragers and cheerleaders. They have loved and challenged me along my journey through life. I am eternally grateful for their investment in me.

Writing a book isn't easy, and it truly takes a village to achieve this mammoth goal. I want to thank Tony Bridwell, who helped me shape the book's structure and clarify the concepts. My editors, Katie Salidas and Shelley Allen, took a dirty rock of literature and polished it into a pearl. Thank you for your talent, expertise, and patience.

To my dear friends and beta readers Eric Littleton, Bruce McIntyre, Bruce Waller, and Gene Hammett, I appreciate your friendship and support more than you know.

Thank you to my parents, for your encouragement and for believing in me from the beginning. Thank you for sacrificing so much to show me the way. Anything I have ever done that is good is because of you.

And to YOU, the reader. I am deeply honored that you took the time to read this book and allow me to serve you. The world needs you to be an Activator, and I hope in some way I have been able to encourage and equip you to make a positive difference in the lives of others.

END NOTES

INTRODUCTION:

1. "The History of the Electric Car." Energy.gov. https://www.energy.gov/articles/history-electric-car.

2. Milenkovic, Written by Milja. "42 Worrying Workplace Stress Statistics." The American Institute of Stress. September 25, 2019. https://www.stress.org/42-worrying-workplace-stress-statistics.

3. Lareche, Willa. "Your Best Employees Are Leaving. but Is It Personal or Practical?" Staffing Agency and Employer Solutions. https://rlc.randstadusa.com/press-room/press-releases/your-best-employees-are-leaving-but-is-it-personal-or-practical

4. Corinthian Colleges, Inc. "Workplace Stress on the Rise With 83% of Americans Frazzled by Something at Work." GlobeNewswire News Room. April 09, 2013. https://www.globenewswire.com/news-release/2013/04/09/536945/10

5. "Workplace Stress." Partnership for Workplace Mental Health. http://workplacementalhealth.org/Mental-Health-Topics/Workplace-Stress.

6. Liu, Dan Witters and Diana. "In U.S., Poor Health Tied to Big Losses for All Job Types." Gallup.com. July 21, 2020. https://news.gallup.com/poll/162344/poor-health-tied-big-losses-job-types.aspx.

CHAPTER 1:

1. Johann Gaspar Spurzheim: A Life Dedicated to Phrenology." Accessed August 23, 2020. https://www.ncbi.nlm.nih.gov/pmc/articles/PMC5493471/.

2. Harter, Jim. "4 Factors Driving Record-High Employee Engagement in U.S." Gallup.com. April 29, 2020. https://www.gallup.com/workplace/284180/factors-driving-record-high-employee-engagement.aspx.

3. Gallup, Inc. "How to Improve Employee Engagement in the Workplace." Gallup.com. August 03, 2020. https://www.gallup.com/workplace/285674/improve-employee-engagement-workplace.aspx.

4. Harter, Randall Beck and Jim. "Managers Account for 70% of Variance in Employee Engagement." Gallup.com. August 13, 2020. https://news.gallup.com/businessjournal/182792/managers-account-variance-employee-engagement.aspx.

5. Bacal, Robert. *Performance Management*. McGraw-Hill Professional, 2011.

6. Harter, Randall Beck and Jim. "Managers Account for 70% of Variance in Employee Engagement." Gallup.com. August 13, 2020. https://news.gallup.com/businessjournal/182792/managers-account-variance-employee-engagement.aspx.

7. New National Study Conducted by Ultimate Software Reveals ...." Accessed August 23, 2020. https://www.ultimatesoftware.com/PR/Press-Release/New-National-Study-Conducted-by-Ultimate-Software-Reveals-Need-for-Greater-Focus-on-Manager-Employee-Relationships.

CHAPTER 2:

1. Pink, Daniel H. *Drive: The Surprising Truth about What Motivates Us*. Canongate, 2011

2. "The Achieving Society | Semantic Scholar. "https://www.semanticscholar.org/paper/The-Achieving-Society-Davis-Mcclelland/ae0d5c4be1a900bebd62351ac1df76747d45d5fe.

CHAPTER 3:

1. "The Neuroscience of Purpose: How Contributing Makes Us Better." Zach Mercurio. May 29, 2019. https://www.zachmercurio.com/2018/07/neuroscience-of-purpose/.

2. "How Our Brains Decide When to Trust." Harvard Business Review. August 16, 2019. https://hbr.org/2019/07/how-our-brains-decide-when-to-trust.

3. Deci, Edward L., and Richard M. Ryan. "The "What" and "Why" of Goal Pursuits: Human Needs and the Self-Determination of Behavior." *Psychological Inquiry* 11, no. 4 (2000): 227-68. Accessed August 24, 2020. http://www.jstor.org/stable/1449618.

4. Sinek, Simon. *Start with Why How Great Leaders Get Everyone to Take Action.* Portfolio, 2009.

5. Ryan, Richard & Deci, Edward. (2000). Self-Determination Theory and the Facilitation of Intrinsic Motivation, Social Development, and Well-Being. The American psychologist. 55. 68-78. 10.1037/0003-066X.55.1.68.

6. Pink, Daniel H. *Drive: The Surprising Truth about What Motivates Us.* Canongate, 2011.

7. Fowler, Susan, and Kenneth H. Blanchard. *Why Motivating People Doesn't Work ... and What Does: The New Science of Leading, Energizing, and Engaging.* Berrett-Koehler Publishers, 2017.

8. Jones, Jason E. "Self-determination theory as a model for motivation in a training context." 2002. Doctoral Dissertation, University of Oklahoma. Accessed August 24, 2020. http://hdl.handle.net/11244/523.

9. Reiss, Steven. "Multifaceted Nature of Intrinsic Motivation: The Theory of 16 Basic Desires." *Review of General Psychology* 8, no. 3 (2004): 179-93. doi:10.1037/1089-2680.8.3.179.

CHAPTER 4:

1. Boyatzis, Richard E., and Anthony I. Jack. "The Neuroscience of Coaching." *Consulting Psychology Journal: Practice and Research* 70, no. 1 (2018): 11-27. doi:10.1037/cpb0000095.

CHAPTER 5:

1. Reiss, Steven. *The Reiss Motivation Profile,* IDS Publishing Corporation, 2013.

CHAPTER 6:

1. "Yoh Survey: Lack of Respect, Broken Promises, and Overworking Employees Are Top Issues with Managers That Would Make Employed Americans Consider New Jobs." Send Press Releases with GlobeNewswire. https://www.globenewswire.com/news-release/2018/10/25/1627089/0/en/Yoh-Survey-Lack-of-Respect-Broken-Promises-and-Overworking-Employees-Are-Top-Issues-with-Managers-That-Would-Make-Employed-Americans-Consider-New-Jobs.html?print=1.

2. Zak, Paul J. "The Neuroscience of Trust." Harvard Business Review. November 27, 2019. https://hbr.org/2017/01/the-neuroscience-of-trust.

3. "New National Study Conducted by Ultimate Software Reveals Need for Greater Focus on Manager-Employee Relationships." Ultimate Software. https://www.ultimatesoftware.com/PR/Press-Release/New-National-Study-Conducted-by-Ultimate-Software-Reveals-Need-for-Greater-Focus-on-Manager-Employee-Relationships.

4. The Impact of Leadership Character on Employee Effort, Work Enjoyment, and Engagement. https://drjasonjones.com/wp-content/uploads/2019/01/Character-and-Culture-Study-Final.pdf

5. Bargh, John A., Mark Chen, and Lara Burrows. "Automaticity of Social Behavior: Direct Effects of Trait Construct and Stereotype Activation on Action." *Journal of Personality and Social Psychology* 71, no. 2 (1996): 230-44. doi:10.1037/0022-3514.71.2.230.

http://acmelab.yale.edu/sites/default/files/1996_automaticity_of_social_behavior.pdf

6. Drouvelis, Michalis, Robert Metcalfe, and Nattavudh Powdthavee. "Can Priming Cooperation Increase Public Good Contributions?" *Theory and Decision* 79, no. 3 (2015): 479-92. doi:10.1007/s11238-015-9481-4.

7. Brooks, Alison Wood. "Get Excited: Reappraising Pre-performance Anxiety as Excitement." *Academy of Management Proceedings* 2013, no. 1 (2013): 10554.
    doi:10.5465/ambpp.2013.10554abstract.
    https://www.hbs.edu/faculty/Publication%20Files/xge-a0035325%20(2)_0287835d-9e25-4f92-9661-c5b54dbbcb39.pdf

8. Gable, S. L., & Reis, H. T. (2010). Good news! Capitalizing on positive events in an interpersonal context. *In Advances in experimental social psychology* (Vol. 42, pp. 195-257). Academic Press. https://labs.psych.ucsb.edu/gable/shelly/sites/labs.psych.ucsb.edu.gable.shelly/files/pubs/gable_reis_2010.pdf

9. Reiss, Steven. *The Normal Personality: A New Way of Thinking about People.* Cambridge University Press, 2011.

10. Reiss, Steven. *Who Am I?: The 16 Basic Desires That Motivate Our Actions and Define Our Personalities.* Berkley Trade, 2002.

11. The Reiss Motivation Profile. IDS Publishing Corporation. http://idspublishing.com/business/

CHAPTER 7:

1. Boyatzis, Richard & Smith, Melvin & Beveridge, Alim. (2013). Coaching With Compassion. The Journal of Applied Behavioral Science. 49. 153-178. 10.1177/0021886312462236.

2. Cialdini, Robert B. *Influence: The Psychology of Persuasion.* Collins, 2007.

3. Waytz A, Mason M. Your brain at work. What a new approach to neuroscience can teach us about management. *Harv Bus Rev.* 2013;91(7-8):102-134. https://hbr.org/2013/07/your-brain-at-work

CHAPTER 8:

1. G.R., Stephenson. (1967). Cultural acquisition of a specific learned response among rhesus monkeys. Progress in Primatology. 279-288.

2. National Bureau of Economic Research Study

3. Durinski, Tiffany. "2020 Engagement & Retention Report: 64% of Employees May Quit." Achievers Resources. May 07, 2020. https://www.achievers.com/resources/white-papers/2020-engagement-retention-report/.

4. Ryan, Richard M., and Edward L. Deci. "Self-determination Theory and the Facilitation of Intrinsic Motivation, Social Development, and Well-being." *American Psychologist* 55, no. 1 (2000): 68-78. doi:10.1037/0003-066x.55.1.68.

5. Baard, Paul P., et al. "Intrinsic Need Satisfaction: A Motivational Basis of Performance and Weil-Being in Two Work Settings1." *Journal of Applied Social Psychology,* vol. 34, no. 10, 2004, pp. 2045–2068., doi:10.1111/j.1559-1816.2004.tb0269

6. Jones, Jason E. "Self-determination theory as a model for motivation in a training context." 2002. Doctoral Dissertation, University of Oklahoma. Accessed August 24, 2020. http://hdl.handle.net/11244/523.

7. Pink, Daniel H. *Drive: The Surprising Truth about What Motivates Us.* Canongate, 2011.

8. Haker, H., Kawohl, W., Herwig, U. *et al.* Mirror neuron activity during contagious yawning—an fMRI study. *Brain Imaging and Behavior* 7, 28–34 (2013). https://doi.org/10.1007/s11682-012-9189-9

9. Duhigg, Charles. "What Google Learned from Its Quest to Build the Perfect Team." The New York Times. February 25, 2016. https://www.nytimes.com/2016/02/28/magazine/what-google-learned-from-its-quest-to-build-the-perfect-team.html.

10. Edmondson, Amy C. *The Fearless Organization: Creating Psychological Safety in the Workplace for Learning, Innovation, and Growth.* John Wiley & Sons, 2019.

11. Rock, David. *Your Brain at Work, Revised and Updated: Strategies for Overcoming Distraction, ... Regaining Focus, and Working Smarter All Day Long.* Harper Business, 2020.

12. Bandura, Albert, "Organizational Applications of Social Cognitive Theory," *Australian Journal of Management*, December 1988.

13. Sauerman, Henry and Cohen, Lesley, "What Makes Them Tick? Employee Motives and Firm Innovation," *Management Science*, Vol 56, No. 12, December 2010, pp. 2134-2153. https://dukespace.lib.duke.edu/dspace/bitstream/handle/10161/4430/285243800003.pdf?sequence=1

14. Zak, Paul J. *The Trust Factor: The Science of Creating High-performance Companies.* American Management Association, 2017.

15. Hall, Kindra. *Stories That Stick: How Storytelling Can Captivate Customers, Influence Audiences, and Transform Your Business.* HarperCollins Leadership, an Imprint of HarperCollins, 2019.

16. Burkus, David. *Pick a Fight: How Great Teams Find a Purpose Worth Rallying Around.* Audible Studios, 2019.

17. Daniel Goleman, Richard E. Boyatzis and Annie McKee, and Daniel Goleman. "Primal Leadership: The Hidden Driver of Great Performance." Harvard Business Review. March 19, 2019. https://hbr.org/2001/12/primal-leadership-the-hidden-driver-of-great-performance.

18. Bartel, Caroline A., and Richard Saavedra. "The Collective Construction of Work Group Moods." *Administrative Science Quarterly* 45, no. 2 (2000): 197. doi:10.2307/2667070.

About the Author

Dr. Jason Jones equips leaders to energize, engage, and activate the best in their people. He is a workplace psychologist, best-selling author, keynote speaker, consultant, and executive coach. He has spent more than 20 years studying workplace motivation and performance and is the author of the book *28 Days to a Motivated Team: A Step-by-Step Guide to Accelerating Motivation and Engagement*

Through his books, keynote presentations, and training workshops, Jason teaches leaders how to become more influential, persuasive, and how to activate the natural motivation of others. Utilizing the latest in neuroscience research, and gleaning from more than 100 years of motivation theory, he curates it all into interesting and practical presentations that are engaging, informative, and entertaining.

Jason has held internal leadership roles in companies in the healthcare, telecom, and technology sectors. He has helped numerous companies build world-class leadership development initiatives and corporate universities. His last corporate role was leading Executive Development at AT&T where his team was responsible for executive education for more than 6000 leaders around the globe and contributed to being named the #1 Learning Company in America by Chief Learning Officer Magazine.

Dr. Jones has worked with companies large and small, including notable brands like American Airlines, AT&T, Ericsson, Seagate Technology, Boeing, McKesson, and IDEX to name just a few. He takes great joy and pride in serving numerous professional associations and conferences each year.

CONNECT WITH JASON AT:

DrJasonJones.com (Speaking, Coaching, Training)
Phone: 214.810.4900
LinkedIn: LinkedIn.com/In/DrJasonJones1
Instagram: @DrJJones
Twitter: @DrJasonJones

CPSIA information can be obtained
at www.ICGtesting.com
Printed in the USA
LVHW090801120221
678799LV00014B/146/J